Speaking
with
Authority

Speaking with Authority

Catherine of Siena and the Voices of Women Today

MARY CATHERINE HILKERT

FOREWORD BY
SUZANNE NOFFKE

Paulist Press
New York / Mahwah, NJ

An earlier version of this book was published by Paulist Press as the 2001 Madeleva Lecture under the same title, copyright © 2001 by Saint Mary's College, Notre Dame, Indiana.

Cover design by Lynn Else

Book design by Sharyn Banks

Library of Congress Cataloging-in-Publication Data

Hilkert, Mary Catherine.
    Speaking with authority : Catherine of Siena and the voices of women today / Mary Catherine Hilkert ; foreword by Suzanne Noffke. — [Rev. & expanded ed.].
      p. cm.
    Includes bibliographical references.
    ISBN 978-0-8091-4586-7 (alk. paper)
    1. Catherine, of Siena, Saint, 1347–1380. 2. Women in the Catholic Church. 3. Authority—Religious aspects—Catholic Church. I. Title.
      BX4700.C4H45 2008
      282.082—dc22

                                                    2008036791

Published by Paulist Press
997 Macarthur Boulevard
Mahwah, New Jersey 07430

www.paulistpress.com

Printed and bound in the United States of America

Contents

———

Contents

Foreword

When Mary Catherine Hilkert's 2001 Madeleva Lecture in Spirituality was first published, it represented a significant contribution in the field of commentary on the life and works of Catherine of Siena. Not only did it address the historically important issue of Catherine's authority within the fourteenth-century church, but it also related that authority and what Catherine herself had to say about it to the public role of women within the church and world of the twenty-first century. It would be marvelous simply to have had that original edition reprinted. But it is an even better gift to have this new edition with its substantially revised and expanded Introduction—an edition well worth having, even if one has read the first!

One knows instinctively from its title that this book, small as it is in size, confronts an area of immense tension within today's church. In many ecclesiastical quarters, the voices of women are not only not heard as authoritative but are not to be heard at all. Hilkert's approach, however, is not confrontational. Like Catherine herself, she is very obviously a lover of the church, loyal in the truest sense. Yet, like Catherine, she is acutely aware of that church's shortcomings and is fearlessly and frankly, but constructively, critical—"unflinching in her passion for the truth," as she writes of Catherine, "but equally convinced that genuine truth can be spoken only with love."

Recognizing that Catherine's vision was limited by the biases of her era and that therefore "her explicit views in some areas must be rejected seven centuries later," Hilkert taps the best and most profound of Catherine's insights, invariably with a careful and discerning eye on the sources. But her attention is never simply on history. She uses Catherine's fourteenth-century life and writings as a lens through which to focus light on today's issues of church polity and practice, ecumenical and interreligious dialogue, justice in society, ecology, and gender equity.

Catherine once wrote: "Truth does not remain silent when it is time to speak…and truth is silent when it is time to be silent."* Hilkert here proclaims the need for "honest speech" and the peril of "unholy silence," challenging today's women to speak with an authority grounded, as was Catherine's, in vocation, wisdom, and compassion. The response to that challenge is seldom easy. In the letter just cited, Catherine concludes by saying that truth, even when silent, "cries out with the cry of its willingness to suffer."

Pope Benedict XVI, as Hilkert points out, has remarked that women "will know how to make their own space," and that a failure to listen to their experience of the Spirit could end in the church's "opposing God." Yet women's experience has demonstrated that the conversation is a difficult one, with as many steps backward as forward. This small book represents a voice of hope on the journey.

Suzanne Noffke, OP
Feast of St. Catherine of Siena, 2008

_____

* Letter T284, to Cardinal Pietro di Luna

To—
Eileen Pentecost, Rosemarie Robinson,
Suzann Strausser, Raphael DiVito, Elizabeth Ann Schaefer,
Bernadine Baltrinic, and Mary Ann Wiesemann-Mills,
all of the Akron Dominican branch of the Order of Preachers—
women who exercised authority with
wisdom and compassion

I wish to express my gratitude to Suzanne Noffke, OP, for her generosity in sharing unpublished resources, for her scholarship and invaluable assistance, and for writing the Foreword to this volume. Thanks also to Mary O'Driscoll, OP, for her writings on Catherine of Siena and for conversations about Catherine's significance today. I am grateful also for the editorial assistance of Kathleen Walsh and Nancy de Flon of Paulist Press. It was a delight to collaborate with each of them.

Introduction

————

Consider the following: A church torn by internal divisions and scandals and in need of reform led by ministers whose lives often fail to reflect the gospel they preach. A world in which the violence of war is fueled by intertwined religious, economic, and political motivations, with factions on all sides lacking courageous leaders who are willing to work for the common good and to call people to reform and dialogue. The survival of whole countries threatened by a pandemic plague and widespread poverty and disease, a burden borne especially by women and children.

A description of the twenty-first-century global village? Or of fourteenth-century Europe and Italy's mystic, activist, and lay preacher Catherine of Siena?

When described in broad strokes, the similarity between the two eras is remarkable. So, too, is the need for contemporary women and men with the courage, vision, and prophetic voice of Catherine of Siena. One of three women named a Doctor of the Church, Catherine was recognized in particular for her wisdom and her "charism of exhortation."[1] Her life and writings serve as a call to contemporary believers—and in a particular way to women and lay persons—to embrace our baptismal responsibility to "speak the truth in love" in both the church and the broader society. Catherine's message was also addressed to church leaders at every level to accept their responsibility for the authentic preaching of the gospel. As she urged in a letter to a prelate of her day, "No more silence! Shout

1

out with a hundred thousand tongues! I am seeing the world going to ruin because people are not speaking out!"[2]

Unholy Silence and Wise Speech in Our Day

In our day, the prolonged silence of church leaders in the widespread sexual-abuse crisis—along with growing economic scandals, power struggles, and failures of pastoral leadership and accountability at multiple levels of ecclesial administration—continues to be reported, and at times distorted, by instant and global communications media. At the same time, prophetic voices and courageous leaders, both lay and ordained, have dared to break that unholy silence, to speak words of apology and lament, to begin to create structures that will bring about greater transparency and justice within the church, and to restore the church's moral authority.[3]

The need for honest speech extends beyond the boundaries of the Roman Catholic Church to other Christian denominations and to the call for ecumenical dialogue among the Christian churches. Among the scandals that the Christian church needs to address in our day are our ecumenical divisions. Four decades after the closing of the Second Vatican Council, the challenge of the opening paragraph of the *Decree on Ecumenism (Unitatis Redintegratio)* remains true: "Such division openly contradicts the will of Christ, scandalizes the world, and damages the holy cause of preaching the Gospel to every creature."[4] Ecumenical dialogues among Christian churches have made extraordinary breakthroughs in the past four decades, but contemporary ecumenical divisions have been further exacerbated by internal church divisions over issues of sexuality and the appropriate ministerial roles of women. Despite painful ecumenical attempts to "speak the truth in love," failure to engage difficult and church-dividing issues jeopardizes the preaching of

2

the gospel. Catherine of Siena's passionate concern for the unity of the church in her day necessarily takes on wider ecumenical implications in the twenty-first century.

In addition to intra-Christian ecumenical dialogues, there is also a clear need for honest and courageous speech among representatives of the religions of the world if religious speech in our day is to contribute to the cause of peace, rather than to add fuel to violence. The role of religious absolutism in fostering violence in our day has brought a new urgency to the call for interreligious and intercultural dialogue and to common religious efforts for peace and ecological sustainability and solidarity. Religious leaders from around the world, including both Pope John Paul II and Pope Benedict XVI, have affirmed that interreligious and intercultural dialogue—and the church's sustained engagement in those dialogues—is a necessity if we are committed to working toward world peace.[5]

Great progress has been made in Jewish-Christian dialogue since the time of the Second Vatican Council, although major challenges remain in that dialogue between two faiths that share a common origin, a complex and painful history including Christian teaching of contempt for Jews, and an ongoing unique relationship.[6] The publication in February 2008 of Pope Benedict XVI's revision of the Tridentine-rite Good Friday prayer for the Jews caused particular concern among Catholic as well as Jewish leaders who have been actively engaged in Jewish-Christian dialogue since the time of the Second Vatican Council.[7] Although the Italian rabbinical association decided to suspend any further dialogue at the present time, numerous other Jewish and Catholic leaders around the world, despite their shared dismay over the prayer's call for Jews to acknowledge Jesus Christ as savior, reaffirmed their commitment to dialogue in the spirit of *Nostra Aetate* (the Second Vatican Council's *Declaration on the Relation of the Church to Non-Christian Religions*).

The recent dialogue between Christians and Muslims also faced serious tensions in the aftermath of Benedict XVI's reference to the negative assessment of Islam and the prophet Mohammed by the thirteenth-century emperor Paleologus in the pope's Regensburg address in September 2006. In the face of the outcries that followed from around the world, Benedict struggled to distance himself from the emperor's evaluation, revising the original text to clarify that he found the comment— or at least its brusqueness—to be unacceptable.[8] The pope never issued a direct apology or regret over the unnecessary inclusion of the citation in an address that was focused on the relationship of faith and reason. He did, however, acknowledge the "understandable indignation" of Muslims who understood the citation to represent the pope's own view, and he expressed regret over the pain the address occasioned. In the revised published version of his address on the Vatican Web site, Benedict explicitly stated that the offensive sentence "does not express my personal view of the Qur'an, for which I have the respect due to a holy book of a great religion."[9]

Two weeks after the original address, in an address to Muslim communities around the world, Benedict also explicitly reaffirmed his conviction that "inter-religious and inter-cultural dialogue is a necessity for building together this world of peace and fraternity ardently desired by all people of good will."[10] Within the month, thirty-eight Muslim leaders from around the world confirmed their commitment to ongoing and serious dialogue for the sake of world peace. Their letter states that

> Christianity and Islam make up more than half of humankind in an increasingly interconnected world, and it is imperative that both sides share responsibility for peace and move the debate towards a frank and sincere dialogue of hearts and minds which furthers

mutual understanding and respect between the two religious traditions.[11]

It goes without saying that Catherine of Siena's fourteenth-century perspective on the relationship of Christianity to Judaism and Islam was limited and shaped by the biases of the time. Her focus on the conversion of Jews and Muslims to Christianity and her support of a projected crusade are criticized in our day even by her admirers, and rightly so. Nevertheless, she was a tireless advocate for peace. She called for frank dialogue and efforts at reconciliation in both political and religious arenas in her own context. Her writings, her prayers, and her own efforts toward reconciliation and peace can be sources of inspiration, encouragement, and wisdom in contemporary inter-religious and intercultural dialogue even when her explicit views in some areas must be rejected seven centuries later.

Indeed, Catherine's concern for harmony and right relationship extended to all of creation. Her exhortation to "cry out as if you have a hundred thousand tongues" is one that is shared by contemporary women and men who recognize the sacredness of all creation as well as the ecological threats that face the planet Earth as a result of human sin. Proclaiming that "God's Earth is sacred," Christian theologians, pastors, and religious leaders issued an open letter to church and society in the United States in 2005. They spoke in one voice about the urgent need for Christians to speak and act "on behalf of all who have been denied dignity and for the sake of all voiceless members of the community of life."[12] Contrasting this gospel mandate of concern for all of creation with the false gospel being preached and accepted in the United States today, they wrote the following:

Ours is a theological crisis as well. We have listened to a false gospel that we continue to live out in our daily habits—a gospel that proclaims that God cares

5

for the salvation of humans only and that our human calling is to exploit Earth for our own ends alone. This false gospel still finds its proud preachers and continues to capture its adherents among emboldened political leaders and policy makers.[13]

The Voices of Women Today

The challenges of making peace and engaging in political disputes, of proclaiming the truth and protecting the vulnerable, of promoting dialogue and preserving creation are struggles that all human beings and nations face. In her own work on behalf of the poor, the sick, and those who were imprisoned, as well as in her preaching and writing, Catherine rarely called attention to differences of gender. But the multiple resources available for social analysis in our day have made it clear that the challenges all of humankind face are compounded for women—especially women who are poor and who face multiple forms of discrimination. The United Nations women's conference in Beijing in 1995 listed twelve serious ongoing forms of discrimination against women. Among them were persistent poverty, domestic violence, inadequate access to education, exclusion from positions of power and decision-making, discrimination against the girl-child, and lack of recognition of women's rights as human rights—all of which are both cause and effect of the silencing and failure to listen to the voices of women around the world.

Five years later, in June 2000, a special session of the United Nations General Assembly addressed the interrelationship of gender equality, development, and peace for the twenty-first century.[14] Although significant progress was reported in many areas of women's lives since the time of the Beijing Conference, the persistent and increasing burden of poverty on women remained. The report cited the following specific examples:

6

- The majority of the 1.5 billion people living on one dollar a day or less are women, and the economic gap between women and men caught in the cycle of poverty continues to widen.

- Women earn on average just slightly more that 50 percent of what men earn.

- Women living in poverty are often denied access to credit, land, and inheritances, and their labor goes unrewarded and unrecognized.

- Women living in poverty lack sufficient access to health care, adequate nutrition, education, and support services.

- Women's participation in decision-making at home and in the community is minimal. They lack the resources to change their situation.[15]

Around the world, women's voices and the voices of children go unheard or unheeded because of the interlocking burdens of poverty and discrimination. The widely publicized systematic rape of women and girls in the Darfur region of Sudan as a weapon of war and humiliation is but one clear example of this reality.

Nevertheless, in multiple contexts and often against great odds, women and girls are claiming their full human dignity and realizing that this includes the freedom to say "no" to violations and threats to their well-being, and the freedom to speak their voice in family, church, and society without fear of recrimination. Women are active in promoting equal educational opportunities for girls, in mentoring younger women, in forming cooperatives and creating opportunities for marketing the fruits of women's labors, in protesting domestic violence and the economic conditions that force women and girls into sexual slavery, in denouncing war and working for reconciliation, and in initiating and staffing shelters for homeless and battered women. Women engage in legal advocacy work, in political negotiations, and even in national and international governance.

Although women are active around the globe in calling for justice and exercising roles of peacemaking, advocacy, mediation, and political negotiation—as did Catherine of Siena in fourteenth-century Italy—a woman is rarely called to do so officially in the name of the Catholic Church, except in the context of a "women's conference." Nevertheless, within the church as well, women are claiming the full dignity of baptismal identity: responding to the call of the Spirit to exercise the gifts they have been given for the sake of building up of the Body of Christ and responding to the pain of the world. Women in Christian communities around the globe are manifesting gifts of wisdom and knowledge in teaching, preaching, writing, sharing faith in small communities, and speaking words of encouragement and hope. Women lead with prophetic voices in pulpits, classrooms, national conferences, women's centers of theology, seminaries, and universities. Women are contributing to the living tradition of the church in creative theologizing from base communities to worldwide gatherings, from meetings of religious congregations to leadership in international theological societies. From home to hospital to hospice, women are exercising gifts of faith and healing. In spiritual direction and retreat centers; in living rooms, parishes, and national and international meetings—women gather to share their gifts and to discern the ways of the Spirit in our day.[16]

Women's "Proper Place" in the Church and the Example of Catherine

Both the needs of the world and the witness of women around the world have led many to raise the question of why women do not exercise more prominent and public roles in the ministry of the church, and, specifically, why the words of women are deemed to be "unofficial" or "unwelcome" in the public prayer of the church. In his first interview with German journalists in August 2006, Pope Benedict XVI was questioned directly about this. When asked whether he thought that women's contribution to the church should become more visible, and whether he thought that women would be entrusted with positions of higher responsibility in the church in the future, he replied that from the beginning of Christianity great women have played fundamental roles in the history of the church. The pope included Catherine of Siena among the three specific examples that he cited (along with Hildegard of Bingen and Bridget of Sweden). Rather than limiting women's witness to rare exceptions, he further affirmed that "in our own time too women—and us with them—must always seek their proper place."

Disputes remain, of course, about what is meant by women's "proper place" in the church and whether any claims can be made about the vocation of all women. The example of the fourteenth-century laywoman Catherine of Siena is cited regularly in those discussions, but Catherine's "proper place" and "true vocation" are interpreted in vastly different ways by various participants. Figures as diverse as post-Christian feminist Mary Daly and Popes John Paul II and Benedict XVI include Catherine of Siena among a short list of examples of remarkable women in the history of the church. Catherine's witness has been embraced by a broad array of groups, many of whom would sharply disagree with one another and with their respective interpretations of the saint's life. The chapel of the Opus Dei–sponsored Catholic Information Center located in the Archdiocese of Washington, DC, is dedicated to Saint Josemaria Escriva, the founder of Opus Dei. Two statues stand on either side of the altar—one of Escriva and one of Catherine of Siena. Yet those who support women's ordination also claim the inspiration of Catherine of Siena, who was so forthright in her calls for church reform. A prayer service organized by the Women's Ordination Conference in Milwaukee opened with another version of Catherine's exhortation mentioned earlier: "Preach the truth as if you had 1,000 [*sic*] voices. It is silence that kills the world."[17] An Internet site that offers a case for ordaining women in the Catholic Church is even more specific in claiming Catherine's patronage. As clear evidence that "St. Catherine felt a vocation to the priesthood,"[18] the Web site points to Raymond of Capua's description of Catherine's childhood desire to be part of the Dominican Order and to share the friars' preaching mission for the salvation of souls.

Another example of different—if not conflicting—interpretations of the implications of Catherine of Siena's life and writings for women today is apparent in the writings of Dorothy Day. Day frequently used quotations derived from Catherine's writings and spoke of Peter Maurin's hope that she herself would be a twentieth-century Catherine of Siena "who would move mountains and have influence on governments, temporal and spiritual." But Day distinguished her own vocation from Maurin's version of Catherine of Siena's ministry in the following passage:

> He would have liked to see in me another Catherine of Siena who would boldly confront bishops and Wall Street magnates. I disappointed him in that, preferring the second step in his program, reaching the poor through the works of feeding, clothing and sheltering, in what he called "houses of hospitality" (where the works of mercy could be carried out).[19]

Even these brief examples demonstrate that Catherine of Siena escapes a single definition and all efforts to claim her patronage in contemporary culture wars, including ecclesial and theological versions of those battles. Her ecclesial obedience cannot be characterized as an unquestioning submission or passive acceptance of authority, any more than her desire to preach can be claimed as a clear desire for ordination.[20] This woman—like Mary Magdalene, Mary of Nazareth, and other holy women in history and in our own time—fits no clear stereotype, and her work fits no clear category of "the vocation of women." She cannot be expected to have voiced all of the hopes of contemporary women or to have addressed the concrete issues that face the church today. But her courageous and prophetic witness in her own time can inspire and help to sustain a similar response to one's unique vocation among women today.

Although Benedict XVI continues to use the language of women's "proper place," he has not proposed a specific formulation of what constitutes women's proper vocation as did his predecessor John Paul II and earlier popes.[21] Rather, at least in his interview with the German journalists, Benedict encouraged a stance of listening to women's own experience and discernment about their calls and responsibilities as baptized women. He remarked, "I believe that women themselves, with their energy and strength, with their predominance, so to speak, with what I would call their 'spiritual power,' will know how to make their own space."[22] Even more striking was the implication in Benedict's next statement that failure to listen to women's experiences of the Spirit could result in "opposing God":

> And we will have to try and listen to God so as not to oppose him but, on the contrary, to rejoice when the female element achieves the fully effective place in the Church best suited to it, starting with the Mother of God and with Mary Magdalene.[23]

The lingering implication that there is a single "effective place" for all women (grouped together as "the female element" in the church) is something that the witness of Catherine of Siena's life and writings calls into question. Nevertheless, the recognition that the church needs to listen to women's experiences of God and of their own vocations is a welcome word from Rome.

That acknowledgment stands in contrast, however, to many of the decrees, interpretations, and actions that have come from the Vatican and some official church leaders in recent years. Issues of concern to many include the following:

- Growing restrictions on lay liturgical preaching (which includes all women's preaching)

- Prohibition of gender-inclusive translations of biblical and liturgical texts for use in the public prayer of the church

- Questions of whether lay ministry is properly considered "ecclesial ministry"

- Denial of the use of church property for gatherings of the Voice of the Faithful

- Diocesan excommunication of members of Call to Action (the excommunication was subsequently approved by the Vatican)

- Characterization of a broad range of feminist theologies as a threat to orthodox teaching or the faith of the church

- Sanctions against women's public speech on controversial issues

- Restriction of "approved speakers" within dioceses or church-related institutions

- Limited appointments of women to administrative offices that require no priestly responsibilities

- Refusal to dialogue with women's groups and lay

groups that are perceived to be "too far to the left," even when efforts are made to reconcile with groups from "the right" that have been in public schism with the Church

- Limits on women's roles in spiritual direction and formation in seminaries

- Silencing any discussion of women's ordination

- Use of one's stance or writings on that issue as one "litmus test" for appointment to ecclesial office or to some faculty positions

The Witness and Wisdom of Catherine of Siena

These were not the concerns of Catherine of Siena in the fourteenth century, nor are they the only issues of importance and concern today. Some might suggest that the crisis in Catherine's ecclesial context was far more radical, even if she did not face the complexity of addressing poverty, sickness, violence, and politics on a global scale. But it is impossible and unwise to rank the order of the challenges of these two diverse eras. Different though the specific situations may be, one of the temptations that Catherine faced threatens many today—the temptation to withdraw from the complicated politics of both church and state.

In times that test our courage and hope, the memory of those who have gone before us in faith can sustain and empower us. This is uniquely true of the memory of the One whose life, death, and resurrection revealed to us that the compassion of God sustains us in even the darkest moments of our journeys. The good news of resurrection promises that the crucified One now lives in God and that his story lives on in the lives of his followers. In the power of the Spirit, that story of love triumphing over death is traced anew in the unique life stories of persons and communities who live in communion with the divine mystery of love that we name God.

In every generation, the Spirit of God, Holy Wisdom, is at work fashioning "friends of God and prophets" (Wis 7:27). Connecting that phrase with the Christian symbol of the Communion of Saints, Elizabeth Johnson has said of the entire "cloud of witnesses" who have gone before us in faith that "their efforts, defeats, and victories empower us for the struggle of our lives to do justice, love kindness, and walk humbly with our God [Mic 6:8]....The living dead become our companions in hope."[24] Remembering the remarkable lives and very real struggles of our ancestors in faith expands our imaginations of what is possible in our day—and what will be required of us. Yet the same Spirit who empowered our ancestors in faith provides the energy and courage for our retelling of the story of Jesus in our day.

Publicly recognized and claimed as a Doctor of the Church, not only for her holiness, but also for her speech—her "charism of exhortation"—Catherine of Siena can be a remarkable companion in hope for women in our day. She was fiercely loyal to the church, yet at the same time an outspoken critic of its corruption. She was sought out by popes and politicians for her wisdom and gifts of negotiation, but she was later dismissed as naive, meddling, and even partially responsible for the failure of her efforts. She exercised a ministry of itinerant preaching that attracted so many to the gospel that confessors were appointed to accompany her on her travels, yet both her preaching and her travels were widely criticized. Catherine's prayer in all its originality is celebrated in our day as mystical wisdom, but even her spiritual director at times questioned it. She was unflinching in her passion for the truth, but equally convinced that genuine truth can be spoken only with love. As a Doctor of the Church, Catherine is noted for her learning, but her wisdom came neither from theological degrees nor from official mandate. Yet this woman presumed to speak in the name of Christ crucified and to dictate words she claimed were words of God spoken to her in mystical prayer.

As we ponder what it means for women in our own day to speak with the authority of the Spirit, whether recognized or not, the witness and words of our fourteenth-century sister can offer insight and challenge. What empowered this woman to speak and act with authority in the name of Christ? What sustained this passionate reformer and courageous disciple? What inspiration can women—and men—called to speak the truth of the gospel today draw from her freedom, her boldness, her fidelity, and her love of the broken body of Christ and of a wounded world? We turn first to the distant mirror of Catherine's life and ministry in the fourteenth century.[25] Letting that mirror shed new light on the challenges of our own time, we will then explore three interrelated aspects of the source and authority of the words of faithful women in every age: (1) the authority of vocation, (2) the authority of wisdom, and (3) the authority of compassion.

One

The Authority of Vocation

Catherine of Siena
in Her Context

The concrete contours of the world into which one is born shape the possibilities and challenges of one's life, the horizon for living out one's unique vocation. An overview of Catherine's context and the main lines of her life and ministry are essential to any attempt to pursue the deeper question of what motivated and empowered her. Catherine Benincasa was born in the Tuscan city of Siena in 1347 in the middle of a century and a country plagued by disease, war, and famine. The dreaded bubonic plague (known at the time as the "Black Death") hit Italy the year after Catherine was born. No one knew either the cause or the remedy for the disease that wiped out large portions of the population of Italy and the rest of Europe. Within years of Catherine's birth, many of the great banking houses in Italy went bankrupt, plunging Tuscany into economic depression. Professional guilds vied with each other for power and wealth, merchants lived with uncertainty, and the lower classes were often provoked to riots and destruction. Throughout Catherine's lifetime, England and France waged the Hundred Years' War and the Italian city-states were at war with one another and with the papacy. Although the popes had been residing in Avignon since the beginning of the century, they continued to operate the papal states through delegates and to be involved in the power struggles in Italy. Florence, the major Tuscan city near Siena, was at the center of the controversy between the merchant Guelphs who supported the papacy and the aristocratic Ghibellines who were anti-papalists. Besieged from without, the church was also in a period of internal decline with many members having abandoned the faith, and respect for the clergy compromised by the corruption, wealth, decadence, and infidelity that marked many of their lives.

Within this tumultuous context, Catherine and her twin sister Giovanna were the twenty-third and twenty-forth of the twenty-five children born to Lapa di Puccio Piacenti, the daughter of a poet and a quiltmaker, and Jacopo di Benincasa, a dyer of wool who was fairly prosperous. Lapa reportedly confided to Catherine's biographer and friend, Raymond of Capua, that Catherine had been the only child she was able to nurse. Catherine's twin sister, who was given to a wet-nurse, died in infancy. Her favorite older sister Bonaventura died in childbirth in 1362. Scholars have commented on the significance that both events had on the extreme asceticism Catherine practiced throughout her lifetime and the significance of her imagery of Christ as nursing mother.

As a child Catherine was noted for her warm and affectionate personality, but also for the strong will that comes through in her letters and prayers as she proclaims even to God: "I will it." In Raymond of Capua's *Life of Catherine of Siena*, he records a life-forming religious experience that Catherine had at the age of six. As Catherine reported to him much later in her life, she saw a vision of Christ on a throne above the Church of San Domenico near her home. Dressed in papal robes and surrounded by her favorite saints, Christ smiled and blessed her. Within a year Catherine had made a vow of virginity as her way of declaring that she belonged entirely to God, a vow she maintained throughout her life in spite of her mother's objections and the efforts of her sister to persuade her to marry.

Growing up in the shadow of the Church of San Domenico, Dominican spirituality and preaching were strong influences on Catherine's life from her youth. In her teenage years she decided to join the Mantellate, a group of Sienese lay women who followed the rule of the Order and lived lives of prayer and service to the poor. Initially this group of widows, all of whom were older than Catherine, resisted the initiatives of this unmarried and inexperienced young woman. But, according to Catherinian scholar Suzanne Noffke, she "argued and connived her way into the order."[1]

After her profession as a member of the group, however, Catherine did not immediately engage in their active ministry of service to the sick and poor. Rather, she turned to unbroken solitude in her room (her "cell") at home, convinced that only in seclusion could she maintain intimacy with God. But her contemplative prayer eventually led her to the disturbing discovery that remained central to her spirituality and preaching throughout the rest of her life. Following immediately on what he describes as Catherine's mystical espousal to Christ, Raymond reports Catherine's insight, in prayer, that God had given two inseparable commandments—love of God and love of neighbor. With this realization that "on two feet you must walk my way; on two wings you must fly to heaven," Catherine turned her attention to the needs of her family, to nursing the sick in their homes and in hospitals, and to caring for the poor of Siena. By her early twenties she had attracted a group of disciples who called her "mamma" and whom she saw as her larger family *(famiglia)*.

Recognized for her gifts for reconciliation by her spiritual director, Raymond of Capua, who became her close friend, she was soon drawn into a wider ministry of peacemaking and preaching. In 1376 Pope Gregory XI placed Florence and a league of allied Italian cities, including Siena, under interdict, an ecclesiastical penalty prohibiting participation in public worship and reception of the sacraments. Since the interdict included the prohibition of trade and the cancellation of debts owed to Florence, it was a cause of serious economic hardship as well as a spiritual penalty. Catherine went to Florence to try to convince government officials to end the war with the papacy and subsequently traveled to Avignon to try to act as mediator with Gregory. While she was there she pleaded with the pope to return to Rome and address the desperate need for church reform. Her peacemaking efforts failed, as did her call for a crusade against the Turks, but her influence did contribute to Gregory's decision to return to Rome.

In 1377 Catherine, convinced that she was called to preach peace and conversion, engaged in a preaching mission throughout the Sienese countryside. By October of that year she had begun dictating her classical work of mystical theology cast in the form of a dialogue between God and herself, *The Dialogue of Divine Providence*, or as she called it, "the book." The following winter the pope sent her to Florence to engage in further peace negotiations between the papacy and Florence. While working on that mediation, she maintained her commitment to contemplative prayer, continued work on her *Dialogue*, and exercised her ministry of preaching by offering spiritual counsel in word and in letter. Catherine returned to Siena the following August, after the lifting of the interdict, and finished the book at a friend's hermitage, just outside the city, by late October of 1378.

Although the interdict and the war between Florence and the papacy continued beyond Gregory's death in late March 1378, peace was finally worked out with his successor Urban VI. Urban had been elected in April 1378 under the pressure of Roman demands for an Italian pope, but there was dissatisfaction from the beginning, particularly among the French cardinals, with his election and his harsh ways of implementing church reform. The dissatisfied cardinals eventually declared his election invalid and elected in his place Clement VII, leading to the Great Schism in the Western Church.

In the face of mounting rebellion, Urban had called on Catherine to return to Rome in November 1378 to support the legitimacy of his papacy and advocate for church unity. He also asked her to preach words of encouragement to the assembled curia in Rome. Catherine spent the final year and a half of her life in Rome, praying for peace, giving direction and encouragement, advocating church unity, and offering her own suffering for the cause of church unity. The majority of her recorded prayers come from this period in her life. She was, however, in ill health and her lifetime of extreme asceticism took its toll. By the winter of 1380 she was completely unable to eat or even to drink water and she was eventually confined to bed. In her last letter to Raymond who had been sent on a mission to France shortly after her arrival in Rome, she confessed that she was no longer sure what God was doing in her life. With the church in schism, she died surrounded by a group of her close followers on April 29, 1380. It is reported that at her funeral her disciple, the Augustinian hermit Giovanni Tantucci, could not preach because of the noise made by mourners and miracle seekers. He is said to have remarked: "You can see that I am incapable of preaching about this maiden; but never mind: she herself preaches about herself most adequately."[2]

The Question of Women's Preaching in Catherine's Era

The extraordinary nature of Catherine's involvement in politics, peacemaking, and preaching in the late medieval period has been noted by many. Catherine also exercised significant public and ecclesial influence through her letters at a time when women were forbidden official channels of communication. She did not exercise her preaching ministry free from criticism or suspicion, but neither was it unprecedented among women in the Middle Ages. A broad movement of evangelical renewal in the twelfth and thirteenth centuries included both women and men who desired to imitate the apostolic life (the *vita apostolica*)

23

through lives of voluntary poverty and the preaching of penance and reform. Women pursued lives of holiness and scholarship in monasteries. Others sought solitude as hermits or anchoresses, or formed religious communities of lay women as beguines. Abbesses preached as superiors of their communities even in joint monasteries of women and men. The twelfth-century Benedictine nun Hildegard of Bingen is said to have preached to clergy, laity, monks, nuns, and ecclesiastical officials—preaching even to bishops and clergy during their synods.

At the same time, the long history of resistance to women's preaching and religious leadership, evident within the biblical accounts of how the first male disciples responded to the preaching of the resurrection by Mary Magdalene and her companions, recurred throughout the tradition. Mark's Gospel reports the initial skepticism of the male disciples on hearing Mary Magdalene's Easter proclamation: "But when they heard that he was alive and had been seen by her, they refused to believe it" (Mark 16:11). Luke reports a similar reaction by the male disciples to the women's preaching of the resurrection: "[T]he story seemed like nonsense and they refused to believe them" (Luke 24:11).

Although Pauline texts such as 1 Corinthians 11:2–16, Philippians 4:2–3, and Romans 16 and texts from the Acts of the Apostles (18:26, 21:9) witness to women's ministries of preaching, prophesying, teaching, and leadership in house churches in early Christian communities, resistance to women's speech is also evident in the letters of Paul and the pastoral epistles. Two texts in particular were cited repeatedly in later centuries to prohibit women's preaching and teaching:

> According to the rule observed in all the assemblies of believers, women should keep silent in such gatherings. They may not speak. Rather, as the law states, submissiveness is indicated for them. If they want to

24

learn anything, they should ask their husbands at home. It is a disgrace when a woman speaks in the assembly. (1 Cor 14:34–35)

A woman must learn in silence and be completely submissive. I do not permit a woman to act as teacher, or in any way to have authority over a man; she must be quiet. For Adam was created first, Eve afterward; moreover, it was not Adam who was deceived but the woman. It was she who was led astray and fell into sin. She will be saved through childbearing, provided she continues in faith and love and holiness—her chastity being taken for granted. (1 Tim 2:11–15)

Not only the passages themselves, but the two theological reasons offered by the pastoral epistle to support the patriarchal household codes of the time, reappeared at numerous points in the history of the tradition as reasons to prohibit women's public speaking in the name of the church: the divine order of creation as revelatory of gender-specific "proper roles" or vocations and women's greater responsibility for sin coupled with their roles as temptresses.[3]

The second-century Coptic Gospel of Mary offers another portrait of the tensions that emerged in the early churches over women's speech and roles of leadership in the community. The text focuses on the competing leadership roles of Mary Magdalene and Peter in the early church, and the question of the authenticity and significance of Mary Magdalene's Easter experience. In that gospel, when Mary begins teaching the male disciples who were terrified by the death of Jesus, Peter challenges both her Easter experience and the authority of her witness: "Did he really speak privately with a woman and not openly to us? Are we to turn about and all listen to her? Did he prefer her to us?" The dispute escalates when Mary asks Peter if he thinks she is lying about her experience. Levi, however, intervenes with a comment about Peter's hot temper and the judgment: "[I]f the Savior made her worthy, who are you, indeed, to reject her? Surely the Lord knew her very well. That is why he loved her more than us."[4] In that text, which was not included in the biblical canon, the disciples take Mary Magdalene's teaching as a source of encouragement for their own mission to preach. But in the centuries that followed, authoritative texts explicitly prohibited women's preaching. The third-century *Didascalia Apostolorum (The Teaching of the Apostles)* and the fourth-century *Apostolic Constitutions* mention Mary Magdalene, but deny that she was commissioned by Christ to preach. The *Didascalia Apostolorum* proclaims:

> It is neither right nor necessary therefore that women should be teachers and especially concerning the name of Christ and the redemption of his passion. For you have not been appointed to this, O Women....For He the Lord God, Jesus Christ, our teacher, sent us the Twelve, to instruct the people and the gentiles; and there were with us women disciples, Mary Magdalene and Mary the daughter of James and the other Mary; for He did not send them to instruct the people with us.[5]

In the medieval period there was a resurgence of interest in Mary Magdalene's preaching apostolate. Her ministry and title as "apostle of the apostles" (*apostola apostolorum*) became popular motifs in liturgy, sermons, art, and popular devotion. The precedent of Mary Magdalene's being the first to be commissioned to preach by the risen Christ was cited in defense of the preaching of women and more broadly, in defense of women's speech. However, the medieval preaching manuals, canon law, and theological writings continued the prohibition on women's public preaching and teaching, citing scriptural injunctions against women's speech. The most frequently quoted texts were the familiar restrictions that "women should keep silent in such gatherings" (1 Cor 14:34); and "I do not permit a woman to act as teacher, or... have authority over a man" (1 Tim 2:12).

Humbert of Romans' thirteenth-century "Treatise on the Formation of Preachers" is one of the classic texts that cited the First Letter of Timothy as support for the prescription that preachers must be of the male sex. Beyond citing the authority of the scriptures, Humbert developed what had become by then a familiar rationale for why women were not permitted to teach or preach. First, because a man is more likely to have under-standing than a woman. Second, because preachers occupy a superior position while women are of an inferior status. Third, Humbert states that if a woman were to preach, her appearance would inspire lustful thoughts in the minds of men. Finally, "as a reminder of the foolishness of the first woman, of whom St. Bernard said, 'She taught once and wrecked the whole world.'"[6]

In his *Summa Theologiae*, Aquinas raised the question specifi-cally of whether women were given a "charism of speech" (*gratia sermonis*), which he defined as a gift given for the profit of others to instruct them, to move their affections to hear God's word and to desire to fulfill it, and to sway the hearers of the word that they may love what is signified by the word and desire to fulfill it.[7] He acknowledged that the gift does belong to women since women can teach as a mother teaches her children. Further, he remarked that the grace of prophecy, which is an even greater gift of speech, was given to women such as Deborah, Huldah, and the four daughters of Philip. He even noted that St. Paul himself referred to women prophesying and praying within the community. Most important of all, Aquinas observed that a responsibility derives from being gifted with a charism:

> It is said in 1 Peter, *As each has received a gift, employ it for one another.* But certain women receive the grace of wis-

dom and knowledge, which they cannot administer to others except by the grace of speech.[8]

Nevertheless, citing the two familiar Pauline injunctions that women should keep silent in the churches and that women may not teach or have authority over men, Aquinas concluded that while women were given a charism for speaking which they had a responsibility to exercise, they should do so privately, rather than in public. Again, his reasoning followed the reasons cited by Humbert and the general patriarchal and hierarchical bias of the times:

> (1) First and principally, [this is fitting] because of the condition of the female sex which must be subject to man according to Genesis (Gen 3:16). But to teach and persuade publicly in the Church is not the task of subjects, but of prelates. Men, when commissioned, can far better do this work because their subjection is not from nature and sex, as with women....
>
> (2) Secondly, lest men's minds be enticed to lust. Thus Ecclesiasticus, *Many have been misled by a woman's beauty. By it passion is kindled like a fire (Ecclesiasticus 9:11).*
>
> (3) Thirdly, because generally speaking women are not perfected in wisdom so as to be fit to be entrusted with public teaching.[9]

Although women did participate actively in the evangelical renewal of the early Middle Ages, at times with explicit ecclesiastical approbation, gradually women's leadership and freedom to preach came under suspicion of heresy. At times, doctrinal disputes and adequate theological preparation to preach were at issue, but it was also clear that lay preaching, and in particular women's preaching, threatened both the social order and the clerical hierarchy. Lay preaching was clearly suppressed by the time of the Fourth Lateran Council (1215) as the unauthorized usurpation of clerical office. Likewise, the beguines, lay women who had adopted a free style of religious life and service based on their religious experience but without ecclesiastical approbation, were suppressed by the Council of Vienne (1311–1312).

Catherine's Sense of Vocation

How, then, in the fourteenth century, did Catherine of Siena become public preacher, papal advisor and negotiator, and recognized spiritual counselor sought out by so many? Catherine did not write extensively about her sense of vocation, but her life, her ministry, and her writings give evidence that her claim to authority was rooted there. Since so many contemporary women also describe the source of their identity and empowerment in terms of their baptismal vocation and their experience of a call to ministry within the church, it may prove helpful to attend to the multiple layers involved in any discernment of vocation, including that of Catherine of Siena. On the most basic level, Catherine shared the call of all human persons to reflect the image of God in which she had been created. That call was in turn deepened and shaped by her baptismal initiation into the body of Christ. Thus she spoke not only of popes, bishops, and clergy, but also of all of the baptized, as other "christs" who were called to be conformed to the only-begotten Son.[10] But Catherine also spoke and wrote of her own unique vocation within the larger body of the church, identifying herself with a tradition of preachers that went back to Mary Magdalene and the first disciples. A brief review of each of these three strands of her vocation reveals that they were interwoven aspects of her identity and the authority she exercised and claimed.

Catherine's reflections on the vocation of every human person to image God were situated within the context of a rich appreciation of the beauty and diversity of all of creation. For Catherine, the whole cosmos formed a "matchless garden" in which the Creator nurtures and treasures each flower in its uniqueness. Within that broader setting of creation, Catherine spoke of the human person as called into a relationship of mutual love with the Creator God. In her *Dialogue*, she expressed her keen sense of God's providence and love at work in every human life: "It was with providence that I created you and when I contemplated my creature in myself I fell in love with the beauty of my creation."[11] Borrowing an image from bread-making, Catherine describes the creation of the human person with the capacity for knowing and loving as a "kneading together" of the divine and the human:

> O God eternal,
> O boundless love!
> Your creatures have been wholly kneaded into you
>   and you into us—
> through creation,
> through the will's strength,
> through the fire with which you created us,
> and through the natural light you gave us,
> the light by which we see you, true light....[12]

Catherine was confident that human intelligence and will were reflections of the divine kneaded into the human. She made active use of both in discerning and exercising her own vocation as well as in discerning God's will for others. She was convinced that when we are living in right relationship with God, our desires reflect the action of God's Spirit within. Thus, she freely acted on her own insights and will in speaking with authority, not only in her letters to others, but also in her conversation with God in prayer, saying even to God, "I will it" or "I want you to...."

At the same time, she was equally certain that human reason and will could be used to deny the divine source of all that is and to resist the call to right relationship with God and all of creation. In their misuse of freedom, human beings introduced the thorns of sin into the divine garden of creation. Because Catherine was keenly conscious of the power of human sin, of its effects on the world and the church, and of her own sinfulness, she regularly pleaded for God's mercy on behalf of sinful humanity, the church's ministers, herself, and those she loved.

For Catherine, the basic human call to image God and to live in right relationship with all of creation was intensified and transformed in baptism. In her prayers, she describes how humankind and all of creation are created anew through the incarnation and redemption of Jesus Christ. Recreation in the blood of Christ crucified, a major theme in Catherine's work to which we will return in chapter three, symbolized not some kind of appeasement of an angry God, but rather the love of God poured out for the salvation of the world. The sin of the human race called forth not God's judgment, but God's mercy. In the face of the horror of human sin, Catherine remarked that God is far more inclined to pardon than we are to sin. Rather than commanding the earth to swallow us up, Catherine writes, God bathed us in divine charity and forgiveness and lavished mercy on us. She describes the blood of Jesus as God's mercy made visible—infinite love poured out—shattering human resistance and turning human hearts toward God and one another. To be conformed to the Word made flesh and blood is to be formed in that same compassion—to share the heart of Christ that is the very heart of God. Thus Catherine writes, we are to "cling to Jesus as a child clings to its mother's breast, finding in his blood the love and intimacy we need."[13]

Participating in the blood of Christ and the fire of the Spirit's love is the vocation of all the baptized, a vocation initiated in baptism and renewed and deepened through participation in the Christian life and, as Catherine stressed, in the sacramental life of the church. While Catherine did not write extensively about the meaning of the baptismal vocation, her writings are replete with references to what it means to be drawn into the life of the God who is "mad with love." Reflecting on the mystery of a God who not only created us out of love, but, in fact, pours out the divine life of love and draws us into participation in divine life, Catherine prays:

> O fire of love!
> Was it not enough to gift us
> with creation in your image and likeness,
> and to create us anew to grace in your Son's blood,
> without giving us yourself as food,
> the whole of divine being,
> the whole of God?
> What drove you?
> Nothing but your charity,
> mad with love as you are![14]

Fundamentally Catherine's authority was grounded in her participation in the trinitarian life of love initiated in creation, deepened and transformed in baptism, and lived out in her ministry of compassion. To put it simply, as Eleanor McLaughlin noted over twenty years ago, Catherine's power was rooted in her holiness.[15] While those called to the office of ministry had a distinct role within the body of Christ, this fourteenth-century mystic did not hesitate to see herself and other women, as well as men, as formed in the image of Christ and called to continue his mission.

But as Catherine's letters to others make clear, our unique gifts, circumstances, and relationships, as well as the specific needs of others and the concrete situations in which we find ourselves, disclose more specifically the unique vocation to which each of us is called. Further, the dimensions of one's vocation unfold and shift during the course of a lifetime. Catherine's call to holiness included a call to contemplative prayer, but not to a monastery, nor to the solitude she would have preferred earlier in her life. Drawn into political negotiations initially through her relationship with Raymond of Capua, Catherine failed in many of her efforts at mediation and was alternately used and rejected by both popes and Florentine leaders. Nevertheless, she remained convinced that she was called to work in that arena even at considerable personal cost. The plague victims, the poor of the city of Siena, and political prisoners she came to know made a claim on her and helped shape her concrete response to the gospel. But in addition to the works of mercy more commonly associated with women's roles and with the ministry of the Mantellate, such as nursing the sick, feeding the hungry, and caring for the poor, she also expressed a desire and responsibility to speak of her experience of God. In her letters she repeatedly spoke with conviction of her call to preach the good news of salvation. But the dimensions of what that call involved shifted during her life, including at various points an itinerant mission throughout the Sienese countryside, personal conversations, letters, sessions of political negotiation, dictating and editing her *Dialogue*, and instructing and consoling the popes and the curia in Avignon and Rome.

Over against those who would separate the political and mystical dimensions of Catherine's vocation and identity, Karen Scott has argued that the two were integrated in Catherine's portrayal of herself in her letters as "itinerant preacher and peacemaker," and even as "female apostle or *apostola*."[16] In a letter to Raymond of Capua in early April 1376, Catherine told of a vision in which Christ bestowed upon her an olive branch and the cross, symbols of her twofold mission as peacemaker and preacher of salvation and Christ's commission: "Tell them, 'I announce to you a great joy.'"[17] The obvious reference to the message of the angels announcing the birth of Jesus (Luke 2: 8–14) carried another connotation in Catherine's day. Medieval treatises on preaching, such as that of Humbert, described the official apostolic work of preachers precisely as an angelic task, citing the same Lukan passage. Yet they presumed or explicitly insisted that preachers must be of the male sex.

Without reference to the issue of gender, Catherine described her call to the ministries of peacemaking and preaching in precisely the same way. She also drew on other images most often reserved to male preachers, such as the sower of grain or the artisan, to describe her own ministry and that of her spiritual family, which included both women and men. Defending their travels and preaching of peace and salvation, she writes to their Sienese critics: "We have been put [here] to sow the word of God and to reap the fruit of souls. Everyone must be solicitous in his own trade: the trade which God has given us is this one; so we must exercise it and not bury this talent, for otherwise we would deserve great reproof."[18] In a subsequent letter she addresses the mounting gossip and suspicion against Raymond and herself by defending her apostolic activity, including her political involvement, with the clear assertion: "Now I declare to you that it is God's will for me to be here." She further maintains that although she had a great desire to leave in the face of the resistance and criticism, "that Truth which cannot lie" declared to her: "To impede much good the devil sows much evil. So go back there and do not fear. For I will be the one to work for you."[19]

In spite of the restrictions on women's public roles in her day, Catherine was convinced that her vocation impelled her to embrace the ministries of preaching and reconciliation. In many ways, Catherine enjoyed unusual ecclesiastical support in her ministry. Still, she located the source of her authority, not in official commissioning by the church or the pope, but rather in her commission by the Creator and her participation in the redemptive sufferings of Christ. Further, Catherine's letters indicate that she did not see this divine source of authority to be a unique privilege of hers since she exhorted other female (as well as male) disciples to trust their calls to ministry. In writing to Daniela da Orvieto, who was meeting resistance in her desire to do what she felt God was calling her to do, Catherine advised her to entrust her desires to Christ who would open up new possibilities—if they were meant to be. In the meanwhile, she writes:

> [I]f you see souls in danger and you can help them, don't close your eyes....Work, then, my daughter, in the field you see God calling you to work in, and don't trouble or weary your spirit over what is said to you but carry on courageously. Fear and serve God selflessly, and then don't be bothered by what people say, except to have compassion for them.[20]

In other letters Catherine explicitly identifies with Mary Magdalene as an "apostle in love" (*apostola inamorata*), and exhorts her followers to emulate her example. Calling attention to the criticism Mary Magdalene also received for her preaching ministry, Catherine remarks:

> If she had paid too much attention to herself, she would not have stayed [under the cross] with those people, Pilate's soldiers, and she would not have gone and remained alone at the tomb. Her love kept her from thinking: "What impression will this make? Will they say bad things about me...?" She does not think such things, but only how she can find and follow her Master....She knew the path [to holiness] so well that she has become our spiritual master (Maestra).[21]

Even though Christ's commissioning of Mary Magdalene had become a focal issue in the context of medieval disputes over whether women could preach, Catherine did not emphasize the issue of her gender in claiming the mantle of Magdalene for her own preaching authority. Nor did she identify herself only with female models of holiness. In a letter to her mother, she explicitly identified her preaching vocation with that of the male apostles, even in contrast to the vocation of Mary of Nazareth. Recalling the gathering of Mary and the disciples in the upper room at the time of Pentecost, Catherine exhorts her mother to emulate Mary in encouraging the disciples to go forth in their preaching mission. But she identifies her own vocation with the call of the disciples to preach and to bear persecution. She explains to her mother:

> [T]he disciples who loved her without measure leave joyfully, and sustain every pain of the separation to give honor to God; and they go among the tyrants, and bear many persecutions....You must know, dearest mother, that I your unworthy daughter have not been put on earth for anything else: my Creator has elected me to do this....[22]

Vocation and Gender—Then and Now

In her own writings, including her exhortations to her followers, Catherine did not distinguish the baptismal vocation of women from that of men. Whether gender imagery played any significant role in her understanding of social roles and in her own sense of authority has been debated among scholars.[23] She did at times draw on the stereotypical language of her day, identifying courage with virility and exhorting both women and men to act *"virilmente."* But for Catherine, "being effeminate" was a weakness in women as well as in men.[24] Whether her entreaties to "act like a man" and not to "be effeminate" reflected an uncritical acceptance of the cultural stereotypes of her day or conscious rhetorical strategy on her part, it is clear that Catherine perceived her own vocation to exceed the stereotypical roles of women in her day. Raymond of Capua, in his admittedly hagiographical biography, drew more attention to Catherine's gender, making the case that she was commissioned to preach in spite of her gender. Clearly Raymond felt that he had to address the issue of the authority of this woman to engage in such a public ministry of itinerant preaching. He did so in the context of the cultural stereotypes of the day, using the same argument that had been used by many medieval preachers to explain the apostolate of Mary Magdalene: God chose to confound the pride of men by choosing a weak and ignorant woman to be the first to announce the good news of salvation. To emphasize the divine source of Catherine's authority, Raymond recounts an early dream of hers in which she described her long-term desire to preach and her experience of Christ's words to her when he commissioned her to do so:

> Remember how you used to dream of dressing up as a man and joining the Order of Preachers in some foreign land in order to work for the good of souls? Then why are you surprised and sad that now I am drawing you on to the very work you longed for from your childhood?[25]

When, according to Raymond, Catherine hesitated because she was a woman, Christ continued:

> Was it not I who created the human race? Male and female I created them. Isn't it up to me where I shall pour out my grace? With me there is no longer male and female, lower class and upper class; everyone is equal in my sight, and everything equally within my power to do.…To humble their pride I will send them mere women, women who of themselves will be igno-

rant and weak but whom I will fill with the power and wisdom of God.[26]

Whether the description of women as "ignorant and weak" is to be attributed to Raymond, Catherine, or both, the witness of her life reveals that she felt empowered and commissioned by Christ and his Spirit. Her decision to join the Mantellate in spite of the resistance of the members of that group, her clear perception of herself as "mamma" in relation to her band of disciples, her political initiatives in the interwoven affairs of church and state, her authoritative letters written in the name of Christ, and her bold responses to God in her recorded mystical dialogue, all testify to the fact that this woman experienced and operated out of a sense of freedom and authority that was rooted in a strong sense of having been commissioned by God.

In the fourteenth century, not only did Catherine of Siena operate out of a sense of her own identity as created in the image of God and baptized into the image of Christ, she exhorted both female and male disciples to do so as well. The irony is that the heightened sensitivity to gender in our day has increased in some ways disputes about whether and how women can image Christ, what the specific vocation of women is, and whether women can speak with authority in the name of Christ or the church. The issue of women's ordination, and the ecumenical tensions related to that issue, have fueled that debate. Underlying that debate, however, are more basic issues of anthropology, baptismal identity, and charisms for ministry—all of which are related to how one understands and exercises one's vocation.

Since the Second Vatican Council, as women have responded to new pastoral needs in both church and world and discerned calls to a variety of ecclesial ministries, the church has witnessed a flourishing of gifts previously untapped in the service of the church. Yet the experience has led also to theological and practical disputes over women's appropriate roles in ministry, including far-reaching claims about the significance of gender in relation to baptismal identity and vocation. When the question of the ordination of women arose in the Anglican Church and as calls for dialogue on that issue were mounting within the Roman Catholic Church, the Vatican Congregation for the Doctrine of the Faith issued the 1976 document *Inter Insigniores*. Along with the well-known assertion that if the role of Christ in the celebration of the Eucharist were not taken by a man, "it would be difficult to see in the minister the image of Christ," came the further declaration:

> [T]he incarnation of the Word took place according to the male sex; this is indeed a question of fact, and this fact, while not implying an alleged superiority of man over woman, cannot be disassociated from the economy of salvation. It is, indeed, in harmony with the entirety of God's plan as God himself has revealed it....[27]

Closely related to the claim that the maleness of Jesus is part of a divinely-revealed plan for salvation is the conviction that the two sexes have distinct roles and vocations in that same plan. Pope John Paul II has developed that view, with particular emphasis on the vocation of women, most fully in his 1988 apostolic letter "On the Dignity and Vocation of Women" (*Mulieris Dignitatem*). In that meditation (as he described the letter), the pope suggests that while both men and women are called to live their lives as persons in communion with others, the two sexes have different personal resources for doing so. Specifically, women received "the richness of femininity" on the day of creation, a way of imaging God that is specifically theirs. Throughout the document, the pope cites Mary as "the new beginning" of the dignity and vocation of women. He includes examples of the roles of other biblical women disciples including the Samaritan woman's preaching, Mary of Bethany's learning from Jesus, and Martha's theological conversation with Jesus in John 11, but his emphasis is not on their ministries of teaching and preaching, but on their "feminine response of mind and heart." The letter also calls attention to the fidelity of women at the foot of the cross in contrast to the response of most of the male disciples, and Mary Magdalene's role as the first to announce the truth of the resurrection "to the apostles." Although the letter includes a reference to Mary Magdalene's title as *apostola apostolorum*, John Paul specifically states that only men—the Twelve—were called to be apostles. In women's roles at both the crucifixion and the resurrection, the pope sees a confirmation of the "special sensitivity" that women showed toward Jesus which he describes as characteristic of their femininity.

Throughout his meditation, the pope stresses that women and men are equal in dignity, but have distinct vocations. According to the pope, women's "personally feminine" vocation has two particular dimensions that are the fulfillment of the female personality—virginity and motherhood. The psycho-physical structure of women gives them a special openness to others and to life. This openness always is related to the covenant as well: motherhood reveals women's call to listen to the word of God with openness and to safeguard the word. Women's special sensitivity to suffering and to joy reveals the special link between paschal mystery and motherhood. However, women can also confirm their female vocation through virginity or their exclusive dedication of themselves to God by virtue of the evangelical counsels. By so doing women realize the personal value of their femininity through becoming a "sincere gift" for God. This form of renouncing marriage for the sake of the kingdom of God is, according to John Paul, a form of "spiritual motherhood."

What the pope identifies as "feminine qualities" are also interpreted as archetypes that apply to men's experience and to the church. St. Paul, for example, used a feminine image to describe his experience of travail in apostolic service (Gal 4:19). So, too, the church becomes a mother both by accepting God's word in faith and by bringing forth new life through preaching and baptism. However, the meditation offers no parallel mention of women's travail in apostolic service or in being prevented from exercising apostolic service. Neither is there any reference to women as preachers or those who initiate new members into the church (although women are described as exercising the definitive role in the formation of their own children). Further, the masculine archetype of representing Christ the "bridegroom" never is applied to women's apostolic role.

Toward the end of the letter the pope reaffirms the Second Vatican Council's emphasis on the universal call to holiness and the share of all the baptized in the threefold mission of Christ, but the text does not make explicit that that threefold mission is a share in the priestly, prophetic, and ruling mission of Jesus. Mary is designated as the archetype for the whole church, but in particular for women, and as the model of the holiness of the church, while Peter is the model of apostolic activity. Having earlier reiterated that women were not called to be apostles, the pope affirms that from apostolic times, there have been women who have played an active role in building up the church through their own charisms. He cites specifically Phoebe's role as deaconess of the church at Cenchreae (Rom 16:1), and the roles of Prisca (2 Tim 4:19), Euodia and Syntyche (Phil 4:2), Mary, Tryphaena, Persis, and Tryphosa (Rom 16:6, 12). The pope remarks:

> St. Paul speaks of their "hard work" for Christ and this hard work indicates the various fields of the church's apostolic service, beginning with the "domestic church." For in the latter, "sincere faith" passes from the mother to her children and grandchildren, as was the case in the house of Timothy. (Cf. 2 Tm 1:5)[28]

There is no explicit recognition, however, that Prisca (Priscilla), along with Aquilla, instructed Apollos in the Christian faith (Acts 18:26), that Paul calls her "co-worker" in Romans 16:3, that Euodia and Syntyche were women leaders whose evangel- izing ministry clearly extended beyond the home, that Tryphaena and Tryphosa were a missionary team, and that Mary and Persis were also involved in the missionary activity of the church. Also, notably missing from the list is Junia (Junias), whom Paul identified in the same passage from Romans as an "outstanding apostle" (Rom 16:7).

John Paul confirms that in every age women have shared in the apostolic mission of the church, mentioning specifically martyrs, virgins, and mothers. He then cites women who shared in the church's mission in spite of persecution and discrimina- tion, including Birgitta of Sweden, Joan of Arc, Rose of Lima, Elizabeth Ann Seton, and Mary Ward. Catherine of Siena is the one woman mentioned specifically as having had a significant impact on the life of the church as well as of society. Teresa of Avila is similarly mentioned for her impact on monastic life. Although not identified as Doctors of the Church, a title they had been given eighteen years earlier, both are designated as holy women who acted freely, strengthened by their union with Christ even in the face of serious social discrimination. But, in the pope's meditation, the prophetic character of women in their femininity finds its highest expression in Mary, the Virgin Mother of God. She personifies the "special kind of prophetism that belongs to women in their femininity"—an openness to receive love in order to give love. The order of love constitutes woman's universal vocation, which is then to be actualized and expressed in women's many different vocations in church and world. The pope ends his meditative reflections by reaffirming that women share in the messianic mission of the church and giving thanks for all the manifestations of the "feminine genius" through the course of history. He remarks that the church asks that these invaluable manifestations of the Spirit (1 Cor 12:4) be attentively recognized and appreciated so that they may return for the common good of the church and humanity.

As is evident in the life of Catherine of Siena, however, this final mention of the freedom and unpredictability of the Spirit in distributing charisms can be in very real tension with the papal emphasis on women's universal "proper role." If a meditation on women's dignity and vocation were to take baptism, rather than creation according to two sexes, as its starting point, the pope's final recommendation that the church needs to recognize and appreciate the charisms given by the Spirit for the common good of both church and humanity would take on a far greater significance.[29]

Baptism, Charisms, and Vocation

What are these invaluable manifestations of the Spirit to which Paul refers and how might they be more fully recognized and appreciated for the common good of the church and humanity? The same question arose at the time of the Second Vatican Council. Cardinal Suenens made a significant intervention in the development of the Constitution on the Church (*Lumen Gentium*, hereafter cited as LG) by calling for inclusion of a section on the share of all the baptized in Christ's prophetic office and explicit reference to the Pauline proclamation that "to each person the manifestation of the Spirit is given for the common good" (1 Cor 12:7). Cardinal Ruffini objected, arguing that charisms were limited to the early church and given as rare gifts, and warned that an emphasis on charism could endanger the institutional church. But Suenens insisted that charisms were neither the extraordinary endowments of a few within the Christian community, nor the prerogative of the ordained or of religious institutes. Rather, the gifts of the Spirit are bestowed lavishly on all the baptized. Recalling the promise of baptism, Suenens maintained that "we all receive the fullness of the Holy Spirit, the lay[person] as well as the priest, bishop, or pope. The Holy Spirit cannot be received more or less, any more than a host is more or less consecrated."[30] Suenens' view won the day on the question of charisms with the Council's recognition that the Spirit allots gifts to the church as the Spirit wills (1 Cor 12:11), and distributes special graces among all the faithful to make them "fit and ready to undertake the various tasks or offices advantageous for the renewal of the Church" (LG #12). The Decree on the Apostolate of the Laity (AA) developed this insight, stressing that through baptism and confirmation, all members of the church are consecrated into a royal priesthood and that with these charisms comes a corresponding right and duty to use them in the church and in the world for the good of humankind and for the building up of the church (AA #3). While it is clear in both the scriptures and the conciliar texts that discernment is required in judging the authenticity of charisms and that charisms are to be exercised in communion with the church and its pastors, there was no suggestion in either the Council documents or Paul's letter that the Spirit's diverse charisms are distributed according to gender.

When baptism and the diverse gifts of the Spirit become the starting point for a discussion of vocation, rather than "unique feminine [and masculine] genius" or special endowments that are perceived to derive from the psycho-physical structure of women as distinct from men, we can see more clearly how diverse the manifestations of the Spirit are in the uniqueness of each member of the body. Catherine of Siena did have a profound sensitivity to the suffering and joys of those with whom she came in contact. At the same time, she was strong-willed and outspoken. She was neither mother nor consecrated virgin in the forms of vowed religious life open to her in her day. Although she was called "mamma" by many, her exercise of her motherhood included not only deep affection and concern, but also critique and challenge. Her desire to be open to hear the word of God in contemplative prayer was matched by her desire to proclaim that word of grace in preaching. She ministered to her own family, but her vocation led her out of "the domestic church" into the streets of Siena, the hills of Tuscany, the city of Florence, the papal palace at Avignon, and the center of the curia in Rome. The vocation of this woman, who had neither formal education nor theological training, included authoring a major work of mystical theology and prayers that speak of God and to God freely in language that emerged from her experience. Long before Catherine of Siena was named Doctor of the Church, her authority was established by the gifts of grace that shaped her own unique personality and that were recognized by those whose lives she touched.

If baptism becomes the starting point for a specifically Christian understanding of vocation, differences of sex and gender remain part of the uniqueness of a person, but not determinative of how one is called to exercise the universal call to holiness shared by all the baptized. In our day we might rearticulate the Thomistic axiom "grace builds on nature" to state that grace expands and transforms the multiplicity of differences that constitute the distinctiveness of each person. All those differences constitute significant aspects of who we are and who we are called to be. But neither gender nor any other single dimension of our personality is the sole determining factor in deciding our multiple responsibilities, whether in church, society, or family. Our relationships and commitments, too, are fundamental to who we are and to discerning what we are called to do. But no single relationship, not even those as significant as marriage or motherhood, exhausts the totality of who we are and who we are called to be in relationship to God. Family relationships are a genuine dimension of our call to holiness, but specific roles and responsibilities within those relationships need to be discerned in each unique circumstance. Even in her traditional Tuscan family, for example, Catherine urged her mother not to cling to her daughter who needed to pursue a genuine apostolic vocation. At the same time, she scolded her brother for not being more attentive to their mother's needs.

How would it affect women's self-understanding and discernment of vocation if we were to take, as the starting point for our reflection, Pope Leo the Great's famous charge to the baptized: "Remember your dignity"? Throughout the tradition, that baptismal dignity has stood in tension with presumptions about anthropology and female sexuality that denied full baptismal dignity and responsibility to women. Hence the long history of disputes about whether women image God equally, or at all, and more recently, about whether and how the image of Christ can be recognized in a woman. But even early Christian thinkers who were convinced of women's natural inferiority, such as Cyril of Alexandria, insisted that the miracle of grace is such that women as well as men are sanctified—"made holy"— through the Holy Spirit; women as well as men become "partakers in the divine nature." In that context, distinctive roles in the Christian community, the family, or the society were determined by what was asserted to provide good order in a patriarchal world view that assumed the natural inferiority of women in relation to men. In our day, however, both the equal human dignity of the two sexes and the universal call to holiness are explicitly affirmed in ecclesial documents. Now the question has become whether women and men are equally capable of receiving and exercising all of the Spirit's charisms, or whether women and men remain "separate (in gifts for ministry), but equal (in the call to holiness)" in the arena of grace.

If we take baptismal identity as our starting point, the baptismal liturgy is quite clear about the question of whether women can image Christ. Female infants, young girls, and adult women are all told by the church as they are robed in white garments "you have become a new creation and have clothed your-selves in Christ." Women know well the baptismal symbols of both tomb and womb as they are immersed in living waters and invited to be conformed to Christ crucified so as to be reborn in his Spirit. Baptized women hear that they are redeemed in Christ, liberated from whatever has held them bound, freed from all evil and demons. How women and men hear that prom-ise, what the demons are that threaten them at their deepest core, and what the journey of conversion will mean for each may differ, but the promise extends to both.

Catherine of Siena wrote, spoke, and acted out of the con-viction that conformity to Christ is conformity to the will of Christ and conformity to the pattern of his life. The promise of baptism is that the Spirit will conform women, men, and chil-dren into communities of disciples who become a living remem-brance of the one who created inclusive communities and open table-sharing, who welcomed children and attended to the needs of the poor and the outcast, who sought out those who were lost or abandoned. We recognize Christ in ministers of the gospel who bring hope to the hopeless, who preach unlimited forgiveness, who bind up wounds and offer new possibilities to those who do not believe in themselves or God's power. To image Christ is to enflesh the life of the one who celebrated life in all its fullness and who exercised mercy even in the midst of his own dying.

One gospel parable makes it quite clear where the image of Christ is to be found: "I was hungry and you gave me food, I was thirsty and you gave me drink, I was a stranger and you wel-comed me, naked and you clothed me. I was ill and you com-forted me, in prison and you came to visit me" (Matt 25:35–36). The disciples in the gospel were not any more adept at recog-nizing the image of Christ than we are, but Matthew's Gospel is definite: "As often as you did it for one of my least brothers [or sisters], you did it for me." The image of Christ is reflected in

the ethics and lives of Christian communities and individual witnesses who tell the story of Jesus with their lives.

At the Easter Vigil, the normative celebration of the rite
includes all the sacraments of initiation. Women as well as men
experience the commissioning of a laying on of hands and the
prayer that they too, like their brothers, will be filled with the
gifts of the Holy Spirit:

> Send your Holy Spirit upon them
> to be their helper and guide.
> Give them the spirit of wisdom and understanding,
> the spirit of right judgment and courage,
> the spirit of knowledge and reverence,
> Fill them with the spirit of wonder and awe in your
>   presence.

Both women and men are anointed with chrism, sealed with the
gift of the Holy Spirit who conforms all the baptized into one
holy priesthood. Aidan Kavanagh has described this anointing
as being "marked or sealed with the messianic Spirit of prophecy,
priesthood, and kingship—being thereby constituted *Christos*—
a 'Christ' in the fullest postpaschal sense."[31]

All those who have been initiated into the one body of
Christ—women as well as men—are anointed by the Spirit to
participate in the threefold mission of Christ. How we are to
exercise that mission—what our individual calls to ministry
are—depends on the charisms of the Spirit we have been given.
Discerning what those gifts are and how we can best express
those gifts is a task for both the community and the individual.
This does not resolve the disputed question of who receives the
charism to become servant leaders as ordained ministers in and
for the one body of Christ, but it does put that question in perspective. All ministries flow from the one Spirit bestowed on all
the baptized in the sacraments of initiation. It is here, Kavanagh

insists, that by baptism by water and the Holy Spirit "one is anointed with as full a sacerdotality as the Church possesses in and by the Anointed One himself. Ordination cannot make one more priestly than the Church...."[32] Quite apart from the issue of gender, it is clear that not all members of the one body of Christ are called to the specific ministries of presbyterate or episcopate. But all the baptized are called to the one vocation all Christians share—the universal call to holiness—or as Irenaeus described it, "getting used to life with God." That one vocation includes and requires the exercise of whatever charisms one has received for the building up of the body of Christ and of humankind.

Catherine of Siena's gifts were many, but she was singled out for one specific charism at the time she was named Doctor of the Church—the gift of wisdom and, specifically, a charism for exhortation.[33] One danger in the public acclamation of Catherine's gifts is that those charisms can be interpreted in a way that distinguishes her from other members of the baptized, and especially other women, so that she becomes virtually "alone of all her sex," to borrow Marina Warner's reference to Mary of Nazareth. But *Lumen Gentium* and the sacraments of initiation promise otherwise. Gifts of wisdom and understanding; gifts for preaching, teaching, doing theology; gifts of offering spiritual direction and wise counsel; gifts of prophecy and discernment— these are bestowed on baptized women and men in every age.

Catherine of Siena's authoritative speech was motivated by her conviction that God was the source of her words; her Creator had elected her to speak and act as she did. A similar sense of vocation motivates women today to prepare for pastoral ministries in which they have very little if any economic or job security, and emboldens women to speak prophetically in the political arena. Others speak of "vocation" when asked why they study theology and develop gifts for preaching and spiritual direction and leading a community in prayer, with little promise that they will be able to exercise those ministries in the context of their own church. Still others respond initially to a mysterious call to ministry that, like Catherine's, unfolds in the course of their lives in ways they could not have imagined. These women do not hold the authority of office within the church even when their gifts have been recognized and called forth by local communities and priests and bishops. But as we have seen in the case of Catherine of Siena, they are empowered by the experience of what they have come to discover as the mystery of God's call in the unique circumstances, relationships, and opportunities of their lives. The conviction that God's Spirit is the source of their ministries sustains the voices of women even when their words are dismissed. We turn then to a closer examination of the charism of wisdom that endowed Catherine of Siena's speech with such authority, her lifelong passion to "speak the truth in love."

Two

The Authority of Wisdom:
Speaking the Truth in Love

In 1970 Catherine of Siena and Teresa of Avila were officially proclaimed Doctors of the Church, the first women to be so recognized for their sanctity and learning. Just three years earlier, the entry on "Doctor of the Church" in the *New Catholic Encyclopedia* had concluded with the following observation:

> No woman has been proclaimed, although Teresa of Avila has popularly been given the title because of the influence of her spiritual teaching; it would seem that no woman is likely to be named because of the link between this title and the teaching office, which is limited to males.[1]

Significantly, on the occasion of proclaiming Teresa of Avila as the first woman Doctor of the Church, Pope Paul VI began his homily by saying, "We have conferred—rather, We have acknowledged—St. Teresa of Jesus' title as Doctor of the Church."[2] Teresa's mystical wisdom, questioned in her own day, did not find its source in that official recognition of her teaching, but rather in the gifts of the Holy Spirit, source of all authority in the church.

The same was true of Catherine of Siena. The authority of the speech of this "Doctor of Wisdom" was grounded in her experience of God and the truth she spoke, rather than in office, permission, or formal theological training. It is true that she did receive a kind of ecclesial recognition of her unique charisms for preaching, mediation, and discernment that was unique not only for a woman of the fourteenth century, but for a woman in any period in the church's history. Not only did Gregory XI listen to her initial challenge to return from Avignon to Rome, he consulted with Catherine when tempted to turn back because of the combined opposition of the Florentines and the French cardinals, and specifically implored her to pray for him. Urban VI requested in writing that she come to Rome to help intercede on his behalf when numerous cardinals rejected his election and threatened schism, and he later invited her to address the assembled curia in Rome at the time of the schism. In his *Life of Catherine of Siena*, Raymond of Capua stresses that Catherine received explicit ecclesiastical approbation for her apostolic travels and her political ministry, but fails to mention that her ministry, her preaching, and her counsel were also criticized and sometimes dismissed by those same authorities. Further, Catherine herself does not appeal to those forms of authority in letters to her mother or closest friends. Rather, she repeatedly returns to her commissioning by her Creator, her vocation as disciple and apostle, and her participation in the wounds of Christ crucified.

While Catherine had great respect for hierarchical authority within the church, she believed all members of the church were called to be obedient to the higher authority that comes from the Spirit's mediation of all truth. She held herself accountable to church authorities, but at the same time exercised her responsibility to criticize the use of authority when it was not performed in truth and love. She felt free to admonish even the pope to the point of advising him to resign if he could not exercise his authority properly:

> My dearest *babbo*, forgive my presumption in saying what I've said—what I am compelled by gentle First Truth to say. This is his will, father; this is what he is asking of you....Since he has given you authority and you have accepted it, you ought to be using the power and strength that is yours. If you don't intend to use it,

it would be better and more to God's honor and the good of your soul to resign....[3]

This woman took it upon herself to interpret the will of God for a pope, explaining that she was compelled by "gentle First Truth." When she challenged Gregory XI to return to Rome, she claimed the authority of Christ Jesus and the Holy Spirit, but expressed her own impatience with the matter as well:

> I tell you, father in Christ Jesus, to come soon, like a gentle lamb. Respond to the Holy Spirit, who is calling you! I tell you: come! come! come!...In the name of Christ crucified I am telling you....Don't make God's servants, tormented with desire, wait any longer. I, poor wretch, *cannot* wait any more. Though I am still alive, I feel as if I am dying of anguish, seeing God so insulted.[4]

Further, on one occasion when the pope expressed his disapproval of her, Catherine maintained that even if the pope were to abandon her, she was confident that the crucified Christ would receive her, underlining again that she and Gregory were both servants of the same Christ. In a letter to her confessor, Raymond of Capua, she asked him to give the following message to Gregory XI:

> [I]f you abandon me, by taking displeasure and indignation against me, I will hide in the wounds of Christ crucified, whose vicar you are, and I know He will receive me, for *He* cannot wish for the sinner's death. And since *He* will receive me, *you* will not drive me out.[5]

Almost six centuries after her death, Pope Paul VI was to recognize this uneducated lay woman for her mystical wisdom and specifically her charism of exhortation. But in Catherine's own day, Gregory XI, the very pontiff she is credited with influencing to return from Avignon to Rome, is reported to have regretted on his deathbed listening to the advice of "meddling women."[6] Whether summoned by popes and politicians for advice or rejected by them as a "meddling woman," Catherine continued to speak and write "In the name of Christ crucified...I Caterina...." Her own authority, like that of the pope and all ministers of Christ, was rooted ultimately in her experience of the truth and love that constitute the very mystery of God.

Her gift of wisdom and her commitment to speaking the truth in love enabled Catherine to offer prudent spiritual direction, to preach the word of God publicly as well as in letters and conversations, to take a stand on controversial political issues, to lobby governmental leaders, to address God in diverse images and language, and to contribute her own theological reflection on the central mysteries of Christian faith in images drawn from her mystical prayer and human experience—all practices of women that are questioned in our own day.

Exploring the roots and manifestations of the gift of wisdom that lent such authority to her speech can empower and challenge women called to those ministries in every age. We will look first at how Catherine's preaching in word and deed reflected the ministry of the female figure of Wisdom in the scriptures. Next we will examine the charism for "wisdom in discourse" for which Catherine was recognized as Doctor of the Church. Then we will turn to Catherine's recognition that the Spirit's gifts—including the gift of wisdom—are bestowed on the many diverse members of the body of Christ, and Catherine's discussion of how to discern genuine wisdom. In each case, Catherine's fourteenth-century insights take on new dimensions and raise new questions and possibilities for women of our day when filtered through the prism of the Second Vatican Council's reform and renewal of the church and the wisdom to be gathered from listening to the voices of faithful women, including contemporary feminist scholars.

Catherine as Doctor of Wisdom and the Recovery of Sophia

In the thirty years since Catherine was named as Doctor of Wisdom, biblical scholars and theologians have called our attention to a remarkable phenomenon that can enrich significantly our understanding of that title: in the scriptures themselves the figure of Wisdom (*Hokmah* in Hebrew), sometimes called by her Greek name Sophia, is imaged and named as female. Catherine's ministry manifested many of the very gifts for which the Wisdom Woman of the Hebrew Scriptures and the Christian Old Testament was celebrated. Further, since it is now widely recognized that Jesus of Nazareth was portrayed as Wisdom Incarnate in the Gospels of Matthew and John, Catherine's fourteenth-century enfleshing of Wisdom adds to the evidence that it is not "natural resemblance" but active discipleship that establishes who can and does image Christ. Even a brief overview of the role of Wisdom in both Hebrew and Christian Scriptures can highlight new dimensions of Catherine's title as Doctor of Wisdom.

Both Catherine of Siena and the Wisdom Woman from the Book of Proverbs were powerful street preachers whose ministries are described as drawing all things together, ordering things rightly, and establishing friends of God and prophets. Like Sophia, Catherine appealed in her own name, preaching truth, abhorring wickedness, instructing all who would listen, offering counsel and advice not only to her children, but also to rulers and lawgivers (Prov 8). The divine delight in Sophia, God's darling child, also found an echo in Catherine's proclamation of God as "mad with love" for humanity. Just as Sophia prepares her table and invites her children to forsake foolishness and grow in understanding (Prov 9:1–9), Catherine invited her children to "come to know that you, eternal Trinity, are table, and food and waiter for us."[7] She describes Jesus, the Wisdom of God, as "the most exquisite food for us" not only in the Eucharist, but also in his teaching. The Holy Spirit serves as the waiter who serves us this teaching by enlightening our mind's eye and inspiring us to follow the teachings of Jesus. The Spirit also nourishes us with charity for our neighbor and stirs up in us a share in God's hunger for the salvation of the whole world. As Wisdom's prophet, Catherine encouraged her disciples to let their souls "grow fat" through active love of neighbor.

Catherine's own hunger for wisdom as well as her mission as Wisdom's prophet are further reflected in the reading from the Book of Wisdom, often proclaimed as the first reading on her feast. The reading of Solomon's prayer for Wisdom and the gift of an understanding heart is particularly fitting on Catherine's feast since it describes both the source of her own wisdom and her exercise of that gift:

> Therefore I prayed, and prudence was given me;
>   I pleaded and the spirit of Wisdom came to me.
> I preferred her to scepter and throne,
> And deemed riches nothing in comparison with
>   her....
> Beyond health and comeliness I loved her,
> And I chose to have her rather than the light,
>   because the splendor of her never yields to sleep.
> Yet all good things together came to me in her
>   company,
>   and countless riches at her hands;
> And I rejoiced in them all, because Wisdom is their
>   leader,

58

> though I had not known that she is the mother of
>   these.
> Simply I learned about her, and ungrudgingly do I
>   share—
> her riches I do not hide away;
> For...she is an unfailing treasure;
>   those who gain this treasure win the friendship of
>   God. (Wis 7:7–14)

Not only do Sophia's ministries reflect the blessings of God, but she herself exercises divine roles and acts with the authority of God in her activity on behalf of creation and salvation, leading feminist scholars such as Elizabeth Johnson to conclude that "Sophia is God imaged as a female acting subject."[8] Thus the remarkable similarity between Catherine of Siena's life and ministry and the work of Holy Wisdom offers a concrete manifestation of what it means to proclaim that women image God.

In imaging Wisdom, Catherine also discloses what it means for women to image Christ since in the Christian Scriptures Jesus is portrayed as a wisdom teacher in the Gospels of Matthew and John and explicitly given the title "the Wisdom of God" in the Pauline literature. Both Augustine and Aquinas, among others, referred to Jesus as "Wisdom begotten" and Catherine herself frequently uses this title interchangeably with "the Word" or "the Son" in her trinitarian prayer.[9] In her own imaging of Christ as Wisdom of God, Catherine exercised a ministry remarkably similar to the ministry of Jesus: announcing the all-inclusive love of the God who longs for the salvation of her creatures, offering rest to the heavily-burdened, befriending the outcast, establishing peace, speaking for justice, exercising a healing ministry, inviting her children to a festive banquet, and drawing all into intimacy with Abba.

Since the work of the Holy Spirit in the Christian community was also described in ways that reflected the identity of

Sophia, it is no coincidence that Catherine's ministry also embodied the work of the Spirit at work in the world as reflected in the sequence of Pentecost:

> Best comforter, gentle host of hearts, delightful
>   consoler.
> In time of activity—calm, in time of confusion—
>   peace, in time of sorrow—comfort....
> Clarify what is unclear for me, revive what is listless,
>   heal what is hurt.
> Make what is inflexible in me elastic, what is
>   frightened in me fearless, what is inconsistent
>   in me constant.[10]

Among the roles of Sophia, embodied by Jesus in the New Testament and attributed to the Holy Spirit in the ongoing tradition, was her call to nurture relationships, to develop bonds of unity among diverse persons and groups, and to draw her followers into friendship with God. This ministry of building and mending relationships and fostering reconciliation in human and political communities was a major part of Catherine's exercise of her gift of wisdom. Too often we think of wisdom only in intellectual terms, when the divine Wisdom Woman and Jesus as Wisdom Incarnate were known—as Catherine was—for reaching out to the poor and extending compassion to those in need (Prov 31:20). The wisdom literature reminds us, as Catherine's life taught her and she consistently advised those to whom she wrote, that wisdom is to be sought and found in everyday life and in all of our relationships and struggles. Kathleen O'Connor has described the search for wisdom not only in the joys of life and relationships, but also in broken relationships, betrayed friendships, failures of community, and even, in the Book of Job, in the apparent breakdown of one's relationship with God: "In the thick of life, at its shabbiest and most exciting, in the routine of daily marketing and in the struggles of ordinary people to survive—it is there that the Wisdom Woman extends her invitation."[11]

Clearly the rich heritage of the Wisdom tradition as retrieved by feminist scholars can expand and ground our understanding of the authoritative preaching in words and deeds of both Catherine of Siena and women called to be friends of God and prophets today. Wisdom's gifts are diverse and plentiful. Some of her daughters are called to preach the word of God whether in streets or in pulpits. Others are gifted with a charism for speaking boldly for justice—"ordering things rightly" whether as administrators in health care systems that are committed to serving the last and least, as lawyers and judges and government leaders, or as political advocates, including those who faithfully write letters and speak on behalf of those who are heavily burdened. Some of Wisdom's daughters are called to the ministry of reconciliation as therapists, advocates, spiritual directors, chaplains in prisons and hospitals, social workers, members of truth and reconciliation commissions, parish ministers, mothers and grandmothers, sisters and aunts, neighbors and friends. Others are called to share Wisdom's delight in all of creation and to help us reimagine what it means to live in right relation with all of God's beloved creation. Catherine's writings and life give evidence of all those gifts. Her letters, in particular, remind us that the authority of women's speech does not come, finally, from political roles or ecclesial position, but from the truth of the words spoken, the authenticity of the speaker, and the relationship of trust and genuine concern that allows one to speak not only words of encouragement, but also words of challenge. Catherine's life reminds us that Wisdom's authority extends from the cosmos to close personal friendships, from political life to faith community to family. In each of these very different forms of relationship, Wisdom invites and empowers her daughters to be prophets who speak the truth in love.

The Charism of Wisdom:
Speaking the Truth in Love

Catherine's participation in the work of Holy Wisdom was so evident that she has been recognized as manifesting the special charism of wisdom that Paul describes in 1 Cor 12:8 as the gift of "wisdom in discourse" *(logos sophias)* and that Aquinas described as a gift of the Holy Spirit that flows from charity. In his First Letter to the Corinthians Paul responds to challenges to his own authority by claiming his vocation as apostle, although he was not one of the original witnesses to the resurrection (1 Cor 1). He further invokes the authority of the Spirit to explain the source of the convincing power of his preaching of the wisdom of Christ crucified (1 Cor 2:1–5). He says of this hidden wisdom of God:

> The Spirit scrutinizes all matters, even the deep things of God....[No] one knows what lies at the depth of God but the Spirit of God....We speak...not in words of human wisdom but in words taught by the Spirit. (1 Cor 2:10–13)

Because wisdom is a gift of the Spirit, it carries the energy and power of God. Later in that same letter in his discussion of the charisms, Paul underscores that the gift is given for the sake of the community and is meant to be used in a way that builds up the community. He also remarks on the Spirit's surprising ways; like all the gifts, wisdom in discourse is bestowed on diverse members of the body as the Spirit wills (1 Cor 12:11). Writing to the Corinthian community in which multiple claims of pneumatic experience were made, Paul stresses that the many gifts of the Spirit find their source in the same God, and that the diverse ministries serve the same Lord Jesus Christ. The final test of wisdom and of all the gifts of the Spirit is whether they produce fruits in love of neighbor and build up the body of

Christ. As Paul reminded the divided church at Corinth: "If I have the gift of prophecy and, with full knowledge, comprehend all mysteries, if I have faith great enough to move mountains, but have not love, I am nothing" (1 Cor 13:2). At the heart of Paul's teaching about wisdom remains the stumbling block that Catherine later proclaimed; the wisdom that they celebrated remains the wisdom of Christ crucified who is the power of God and the wisdom of God (1 Cor 1:22–24).

Thomas Aquinas drew on both the Book of Wisdom and First Corinthians in discussing wisdom as one of the seven gifts of the Holy Spirit. He described the seven gifts as going beyond the virtues that flow from the life of grace to a kind of genuine affinity with the ways of God that flows from friendship with God. In discussing the gift of wisdom he cited both Paul's reminder that the Spirit gives gifts as the Spirit chooses (1 Cor 12:8–11) and the Book of Wisdom's portrayal of the most fundamental work of Wisdom: "[I]n each generation she passes into holy souls, she makes them friends of God and prophets" (Wis 7:27).[12] As Thomas described it, wisdom is the gift that gives one a knowledge of God that flows from love and a discerning judgment that allows one to see persons and situations as God sees them. This kind of knowing goes beyond the realm of concepts and study to the way we know our friends. It is, Aquinas says, a knowing that is, as it were, "tasted" or a "knowledge by compassion."[13] This experiential knowledge born of love judges according to divine truth. Aquinas agreed with Paul that this kind of wisdom is available only through union with Christ in the power of Holy Spirit ("the Word breathing love"). Like Paul, Thomas remained convinced that the wisdom of God reaches its fullest revelation in the crucified Christ, as his own commentary on 1 Corinthians demonstrates. In Christ who is wisdom begotten and infinite love poured out, truth and love are inseparable. As a share in that twofold gift, the charism of wisdom, according to Aquinas, enables one not only to make wise judgments, but to direct others in doing so. It also empowers one to preach with wisdom, to teach with knowledge born of love, and to engage in peacemaking with compassion.

Catherine of Siena gave evidence of her gift of wisdom in exactly those ministries. The energy and dynamism of the Spirit's charisms, that both Paul and Aquinas recognized, come through even in her letters where she often describes herself as "compelled to speak." She asks forgiveness for her boldness, but asserts that she speaks out of the fullness of her heart and out of concern for those to whom she writes. That her preaching moved her hearers to conversion and action is beyond doubt. She was even assigned a trio of confessors to celebrate the sacrament of reconciliation with her hearers because the power of her words was so widely recognized. As Raymond of Capua described God's promise to her at the time of her own commissioning to preach: "I will give you a mouth and a wisdom which none shall be able to resist."[14]

The source of the authority of Catherine's words and the source of all wisdom and good judgment are clearly identified in both her *Dialogue* and her prayers. Using language very similar to that of Augustine, Aquinas, and a number of the mystics, Catherine speaks of a knowledge of God's love that goes beyond a recognition of God's blessings in one's life to the knowledge that belongs to those who have been made friends of God. She says of this experience of God's love: "Beyond the knowledge of ordinary love, these taste it and know it and experience it and feel it in their very souls."[15] In her prayers and letters Catherine uses extravagant language of drinking God's love and being inebriated by it, of lovers and spousal union, of being "crazy with love."

Her mystical experience moved her to speak freely to God and of God in multiple images and names. Catherine regularly spoke to and of the Trinity in the classical language of Father, Son, and Spirit. But that language did not limit her imagination in expressing her experience of God that exceeded and broke

64

open all human categories. In a single passage in her *Dialogue* she could refer to God as "the Father" and "the Son" and speak of "nursing at the breast of the crucified." In other passages she speaks of the Spirit, too, as a mother who nurses us at the breast of divine charity and writes of Christ as our "foster mother." Catherine also drew freely on nature images in naming God "O deep sea," "O light surpassing all other light," "O abyss," "O fire ever-blazing." She used language that sounds abstract and philosophical in intimate address: "Godhead!" "O supreme eternal Good," "O Truth," "O Eternal God," "O Charity," "O Eternal Wisdom," "O Trinity." In her prayer as in her life, Catherine was both solidly rooted in the tradition and open to new and creative impulses of the Spirit. In our day, her mystical wisdom remains a challenge both to those who would eliminate language of God as Father, Son, and Spirit, and to those who insist that only those names constitute appropriate trinitarian speech or address for God. Catherine's prayers and her *Dialogue* give evidence that she knew from experience that multiple ways of naming God disclose different aspects of the one mystery that is beyond all names.

As Catherine herself learned and taught, the measure of the authenticity of prayer is to be found in its fruits. Thus she consistently connected her mystical experience with love of neighbor, hunger for salvation of the whole world, feasting at the table of the cross, and compassion for the suffering and the sinful. She also described her experiences of darkness and the absence of God. Catherine's experience of God's own wisdom led not only to unspeakable joy, but also to tears, lament, and a ministry of preaching conversion and reconciliation in the name of Christ crucified.

That ministry required not only the exercise of God's compassion, but a fearless speaking of God's truth. Catherine describes the focus of her ministry and life in the opening paragraph of her *Dialogue:* "And loving, she seeks to pursue the truth and clothe herself in it." The inseparable link between the Spirit of God, whom Catherine most frequently identifies as "Love" or "Mercy," and the Word or Wisdom of God, whom Catherine usually refers to as "Truth," undergirds the pattern of her life and her exhortations. Genuine love and concern for the common good require that we speak the truth, but truth can be expressed fully only in love.

Catherine's passion for the truth and her conviction that the good of others, the unity of the church, and the reconciliation of political factions required it, empowered her bold speech. Her fidelity to the truth was at the heart of the authority of Catherine's words. She spoke of being a lover of the truth and a spouse of the truth. That identity and relationship gave her what she considered a mandate to speak the truth without fear of consequences (which in her case included an assassination attempt!). Thus she wrote to Urban VI that she and her followers would proclaim the truth "wherever it pleases God's will, even to your holiness."[16] Earlier, in writing to Gregory XI, she censured those who held authority in the church for their self-centeredness and their fear of displeasing others:

> They are forever afraid of offending and making enemies—and all of this because of self-love. Sometimes it's just that they would like to keep peace, and this, I tell you, is the worst cruelty one can inflict. If a sore is not cauterized or excised when necessary, but only ointment is applied, not only will it not heal, but it will infect the whole [body], often fatally....[17]

In her *Dialogue* she writes of God's rebuke of clergy and religious for their extravagant lives, misuse of money, sensuality, pride, infidelity to prayer, and lack of concern for the poor. While they were meant to exercise authority as the good shepherd did, to minister as angels, and to be "fragrant flowers" in the larger garden of the church, in Catherine's assessment, they were instead wolves, devils incarnate, and stinking weeds.[18]

Thus she wrote to Gregory XI with strong words about his choice of pastors and cardinals:

> You are in charge of the garden of holy church. So uproot from that garden the stinking weeds full of impurity and avarice, and bloated with pride (I mean the evil pastors and administrators who poison and corrupt the garden)....Tell them to tend to administering themselves by a good holy life. Plant fragrant flowers in this garden for us, pastors and administrators who will be true servants of Jesus Christ crucified, who will seek only God's honor and the salvation of souls, who will be fathers to the poor.[19]

She was equally frank with political leaders. When the magistrates who governed the republic of Lucca were deciding to side with the antipapal league of Milan and Florence, Catherine tried to intervene:

> Don't give in to any fear of losing your peace or your status, and don't be influenced by any threats these devils might make....You should know that if you were to [join the antipapal league] to save yourselves and have peace, you would fall into greater warfare and ruin than ever—physically as well as spiritually. Don't get involved in such stupidity![20]

She tried to persuade Charles V, the king of France, to support the papacy as well. In a letter to him in 1376 she did not hesitate to offer her critique of the war France was waging with England, as well as her assessment of how he should govern. After reminding him that his wealth, status, and power were only "on loan" and that he should act as a wise steward of all he had been given, she continued:

> The second thing I am asking is that you uphold true holy justice. Let it not be adulterated by selfish love for yourself or by flattery or by human respect. And don't pretend not to see if your officials are inflicting injustice for money, denying the poor their rights.... No more, for the love of Christ crucified! Don't you realize that you are the cause of this evil if you don't do what you can?[21]

While Catherine spoke the truth as she saw it in every arena and to each person to whom she wrote, she felt a particular responsibility to do so in relation to those she most loved. She wrote to her brother, calling him to task for not attending to the needs of their mother. Although he was having financial difficulties, which she acknowledged and expressed concern about, she remarked that even if he could not offer financial assistance, he could at least keep in touch with his own mother. She penned the following challenge to him:

> Oh ingratitude! You've thought nothing of the pains of childbirth or the milk she gave you from her breast or all her trouble over you and the others. And if you tell me, "She had no concern for us!" I say, "Not so!" In fact, she was so concerned about you and your brother that it cost her most dearly. But let's suppose it were true— it is you who are obligated to her, not she to you. She didn't take *your* flesh, but gave you hers.[22]

Not only family commitments, but also the ministry of friendship, in Catherine's estimation, required speaking the truth to those we have been given to love "with a special love." Thus she spoke her mind to her friends, both male and female. She celebrated the gift of their friendship, but at the same time exhorted them to greater trust and courage, advising even her spiritual director on prayer and calling for a bolder exercise of gifts on the part of her friends, even in the face of adversity.

But whether writing to pope, politician, disciple, family member, or friend, Catherine always placed even her strongest critiques in the context of love, concern, and the possibility of conversion. In her letters to the popes she expressed her respect for the office entrusted to them as vicar of Christ and her desire that they indeed would rule as Christ did. In one of her most creative ways of making this point, Catherine drew on her favorite food imagery. She actually prepared a candied orange for Pope Urban VI, which she sent to him along with the recipe that called for replacing bitterness with an edible bitter-sweetness. As Karen Scott has described Catherine's allegorical explanation of how the steps in the recipe parallel the necessary steps in the pope's conversion: "Caterina's gift of the candied orange is an elaborate representation of what Urban's soul will be like once the divine Cook is finished with him."[23] She encouraged the popes and other leaders to win over their enemies with love, to "catch them with the hook of love," and to use kindness to conquer malice.

According to Catherine's *Dialogue*, God's compassion and care are to guide those who are responsible for guiding others, whether in exercising political or ecclesiastical authority or in confronting a family member or friend. She remarks there that wise religious superiors love those entrusted to their care and put up with the burden of their shortcomings. At the end of her extended reflections on the corruption among clergy and religious, she concludes that God's word is calling her to pray and work for the conversion of those of whom she is critical: "You ought to despise and hate the minister's sins and try to dress them in the new clothes of charity and holy prayer, and wash away their filth with your tears."[24] At several points in the text

Catherine uses the image of "snatching the rose from the thorns" to describe how to call forth the best in others and how to look for the good in the most difficult of situations.

Seeking Wisdom Together:
The Need for Many Voices

Part of the reason that Catherine was so insistent on the responsibility of all members in the body of Christ to speak the truth in love was that she was convinced that no one member, not even the pope, had full access to the truth, which rests in God alone. Reflecting on that in her dialogue with God, Catherine came to the insight that God has given unique gifts to each member of the body of Christ. No one member has all the gifts necessary for the life of that body precisely so that we would realize our interdependence. Speaking with the authority of God's voice, she writes:

> The same is true of many of my gifts and graces, virtue and other spiritual gifts, and those things necessary for the body and human life. I have distributed all in such a way that no one has all of them. Thus have I given you reason—necessity, in fact—to practice mutual charity. For I could well have supplied each of you with all your needs, both spiritual and material. But I wanted to make you dependent on one another so that each of you would be my minister, dispensing the graces and gifts you have received from me....So you see, I have made you my ministers, setting you in different positions and in different ranks to exercise the virtue of charity. For there are many rooms in my house.[25]

This necessary interdependence extended not only to serving as ministers of charity to one another, but also to serving as ministers of truth or wisdom. Catherine held church leaders in high regard in spite of whatever limitations and even sinfulness she observed and addressed. She respected the fact that they were entrusted with a unique office and responsibility. Yet precisely for that reason she argued that they were in need of consultation and discernment in discovering the truth of God's will for the church. Suzanne Noffke has observed that Catherine always used the term "minister" rather than "teacher" of truth when referring to pastors and to the church itself. She has remarked that, for Catherine, "the Church and its leaders are only servants of truth in whose name they command and teach: Christ alone is called the teacher or master of truth."[26] Catherine exercised her own gift of wisdom not only in offering wise counsel, or asking the difficult question, but also in exhorting persons and groups in conflict—including those within the church—to listen to one another.

Catherine's hierarchical view of the church was far from a twentieth-century egalitarian democracy, and she repeatedly declared her own obedience to the pope as vicar of Christ, remarking that even if he were the "devil incarnate, I must not defy him."[27] At the same time, her conviction that no one member of the body was given all the gifts necessary for the good of the body as a whole extended to the pope and his ministry as well. On that basis, Catherine proposed that Pope Urban VI should have a "council of the servants of God" in addition to his cardinals and political advisors because while he had authority over the entire church, he had only one man's vision. She further advised the pope on the importance of exercising his authority with patience and of listening to the wisdom of those who offered criticism of the abuses in the church. She warned that otherwise he might make mistakes of judgment that they could have spared him:

> Oh most holy father, be patient when people talk to
> you about these things, for they speak only for God's

honor and your well-being, as children must do when they tenderly love their father....[T]hey are well aware that their father has a huge family to care for, yet has only one man's vision....So if his trueborn children were not concerned enough to watch out for their father's honor and interests he would often be deceived. And so it is [with you]....So far as authority is concerned you can do everything, but in terms of vision, you can see no more than any one person can....And I know that your holiness really wants helpers who *will* help you, but you have to be patient in listening to them![28]

Catherine's image of magisterial teaching and learning as that of a parent listening to children is clearly not a model that is adequate to foster adult participation and responsibility grounded in the equal dignity, but diverse roles, of the baptized into the one body of Christ. At the same time, even in her fourteenth-century hierarchical context, which still identified diverse roles as differences of rank, she highlighted the diversity of charisms, multiple gifts of insight, and responsibilities for voicing those insights. Six centuries later, her call for the exercise of authority to be grounded in consultation and listening to the wisdom of the whole community was echoed at the Second Vatican Council, but that call has yet to be implemented structurally in the workings of the church at every level.

While Catherine did not focus specifically on gender in exhorting the pope, cardinals, and clergy to listen to the voices of those who offer criticism and alternative insights to the leaders of the church, it is clear from her own writings and her letters to others that women's voices were to be included as sources of potential insight, wisdom, and even correction. In our day, in spite of Pope John Paul's appeal to all of the institutions of the church at the time of the Beijing World Conference on Women to welcome the contribution of the women of the church to new forms of leadership in service, no corresponding structures were proposed or developed to achieve that goal. Serious efforts have been made at the level of individual pastors, bishops, and even some bishops' conferences, but many of those same efforts have met with resistance at the level of the Vatican. The idea that any woman would be summoned to Rome to give counsel to a pope (let alone that a pope should come to her to seek her counsel as Gregory did with Catherine) is clearly beyond the imagination of those who criticize bishops even for listening to women. At the end of the fated attempt at issuing a U.S. Bishops' Pastoral on Women's Concerns, the late Bishop P. Francis Murphy revealed that the very process of consultation was the issue that raised the most concern about the pastoral among Vatican officials: "They asserted that bishops are teachers, not learners; truth cannot emerge through consultation."[29]

Six centuries after her death, Catherine's gifts for wisdom and exhortation and her public exercise of those gifts for the sake of the church have been publicly announced and celebrated. But the gifts of her sisters in the twentieth and twenty-first centuries have not been equally welcome. The unlettered Catherine was acclaimed as Doctor of the Church for her mystical wisdom, yet no woman has yet been named as a member of the International Theological Commission. Rarely are women asked to serve as theological advisors to bishops or bishops' conferences except, at times, on issues that are considered "women's issues," in spite of the fact that women on every continent now hold doctoral degrees in theology, including pontifical degrees. Catherine was summoned to Genoa and to Rome to counsel popes, yet canon law and documents for priestly formation in our day rule out the possibility of a woman serving as a spiritual director for seminarians. Catherine's preaching and teaching of the word inspired paupers, popes, and politicians. We are in the midst of an evangelical renewal in our own day when numerous qualified lay women and lay men express a desire to share more fully in the church's preaching ministry, and some bishops work to foster qualified lay preaching. Yet Vatican documents in recent years maintain that it is the priest who is properly "teacher of the Word," and that "proclaiming the Gospel is a ministry deriving from the sacrament of orders."[30]

Catherine is hailed for her loyalty to the church in spite of her strong criticism of cardinals and corrupt clerics and her challenge to the pope to resign if he could not exercise his authority for the good of the whole church. Yet in 1979, when Sister Theresa Kane, RSM, who was at that time President of the Leadership Conference of Women Religious (LCWR), included the following statement in her two-page welcome message to the pope, her loyalty to the church was questioned by many:

> As I share this privileged moment with you, Your Holiness, I urge you to be mindful of the intense suffering and pain which is part of the life of many women in these United States. I call upon you to listen with compassion and to hear the call of women who comprise half of humankind. As women we have heard the powerful messages of our Church addressing the dignity and reverence for all persons. As women we have pondered these words. Our contemplation leads us to state that the Church in its struggle to be faithful to its call for reverence and dignity for all persons must respond by providing the possibility of women as persons being included in all ministries of our Church.[31]

Kane's welcome began with greetings of "profound respect, esteem and affection" from women religious throughout the country. She spoke of the inspiration of the pope's spirit of courage, his calls to attend to the needs of the poor and the oppressed, and his challenges to the United States to respond to the cry of the poor. She assured the pope of the prayers, support, and fidelity of women religious "as you continue to challenge us to be women of holiness for the sake of the kingdom," and she closed with a prayer for the pope citing the words of the Magnificat. Nevertheless, in open letters, public apologies, and editorials, she was accused of "impertinence," "public disgrace," "wounding and dividing the Church," "perverting the Church's teaching," "repudiating the Holy Spirit," and "being like the woman in the Garden who demands to have the 'forbidden fruit' so she will have her own will and 'be like God.'"[32] Both Catherine of Siena and Theresa Kane faced the rare opportunity and responsibility to speak publicly to a pope for the sake of the church. Each spoke her understanding of the truth in love. (Kane chose that very phrase—"To Speak the Truth in Love"— as the title of her presidential address to the LCWR the following August in Philadelphia.) While their words inspired hope for many, their motives and wisdom were questioned by others. Neither could know at the time the impact her words and her courage would have on the history of the church.

At the heart of Kane's plea was a call that went beyond the specifics of women's ministries, a call to listen with compassion to the voices of women. Like Catherine's proposal for a "council of the servants of God," this call to listen rests on Paul's confidence that all the parts of the body, diverse though they may be, need each other. Specifically, in terms of decision-making, a collegial, collaborative, and consultative mode of exercising magisterial authority flows from the conviction not only that individual charisms are given for the sake of the common good, but also that the Spirit has bestowed the gift of wisdom on the body of believers as a whole. Vatican II described this gift as a *sensus fidei* (sense of faith)—an instinct for the authentic faith of the church that is available only through a process of discernment that attempts to measure the authentic *sensus fidelium* (sense of the faithful). This does not refer to something that can be determined easily by polls or majority vote, but rather to a process whereby faithful believing communities—including faithful women—articulate their experiences of where the Spirit is leading the church. Jean-Marie Tillard describes this kind of corporate sense of faith or affinity for the truth using the same language that Aquinas used to describe the gift of wisdom—a "knowledge of God springing from a communion in friendship, from the intuition which the experience of the Spirit arouses."[33]

The notion that the community of the baptized has a graced affinity for "right teaching" is part of a long-standing, but little emphasized, tradition in the church. If the Spirit of Truth does indeed arouse and sustain a "sense of faith" in the community of believers, then that experience—including the experience of believing women—cannot be ignored. Women do not speak in one voice, nor should we, but our multiple experiences are part of the church's living tradition and have a contribution to make to the authentic teaching of the church. But the worldwide church has yet to develop viable structures that would promote the exercise of this discernment of the authentic and living faith of the church among the baptized.

Without attending specifically to the experience of women, Avery Dulles has raised cautions about appeals to the *sensus fidelium* in our day. He observes that the very notion of "universal consent" is unthinkable in our day and age. In addition, he notes that authentic faith is sometimes preserved by a "faithful remnant" or a "privileged vanguard," rather than by the majority of believers. Further, he comments that nearly every authentic development when it first appears on the scene meets with initial resistance. Doctrinal and moral issues in our day require some degree of theological education and the complexities of doctrine cannot always be judged by "uninformed public opinion." Finally, Dulles cautions that Christians are members not only of the church, but also of secular society; thus there is always the danger of "tailoring the Gospel to fit the accepted postulates of their own social group."[34]

Dulles's points are all valid concerns. But, if anything, they highlight the need for processes of genuine listening and discernment that include the diverse voices of women. The charge is frequently made that a destructive and secular form of "radical feminism" is the driving force behind voices and movements of protest over women's role in the church. However, the faithful remnant at the foot of the cross were a company of women accompanied by the Beloved Disciple, and the privileged vanguard who announced the news of the resurrection was composed of Mary Magdalene and her companions. So too it is possible that faithful women and men who are proposing wider roles for women in the church and structural changes within the church constitute part of that privileged vanguard in our day. As Vatican II recognized, not everything that the church has taught in the past constitutes part of its authentic tradition. Discerning what should be preserved and what changed in our day is precisely the issue, and as Dulles rightly notes, resistance accompanies the inevitable process of change. Doctrinal and moral disputes do require the wisdom of those who are theologically trained as well as the wisdom that comes from the broader community of believers. But the further question needs to be raised as to whose interpretations and theological judgments are included when decisions and statements are made about women's roles, vocations, and ethical responsibilities. Finally, while forms of "secular feminist ideology" can be a bias affecting the judgment of believers, so also are patriarchy and clericalism forms of bias that affect the judgment of the church. We all remain finite and sinful, both as individuals and as communities of faith. We do stand in need of the Spirit's conversion and of one another's critique and speaking the truth in love. But for that to happen and to benefit the whole church, we need genuine opportunities to speak and to listen and structures that facilitate and secure freedom for that kind of truthful speech. Here Catherine's approach to the question of discerning the truth can prove instructive.

Discerning the Truth

Catherine's writings on discretion or discernment focus on prudential judgments of individuals and growth in the spiritual life, rather than on ecclesial processes of communal discernment.[35] But, several aspects of Catherine's work suggest that the two are closely related. What she has written about the courage required to know and follow truth has implications for the church as a whole in its search for truth and its teaching of truth as well as for individual believers. First, there is Catherine's fundamental insight that God alone is "First Truth"; she frequently addresses both God and Christ as *Prima Verita* and *prima dolce Verita* (sweet or gentle Truth). Truth itself rests in God alone; thus it is the Spirit who instructs the church in truth. Second, as servants of the truth and ministers to the truth, those who are official teachers within the church are called to be "persons who are in love with truth and enlightened by it—not persons who are insensitive to and ignorant of it."[36] Third, Catherine remained convinced that it was every Christian's responsibility to "pursue truth and clothe herself in it" as well as to speak the truth courageously regardless of the cost.

In Catherine's view, discernment requires not only love of truth, but also honest self-knowledge, which is inseparable from knowledge of God. This in turn requires the kind of humility that includes acknowledgment of one's gifts and the responsibilities that flow from those gifts, as well as awareness of one's limitations and failings. Catherine's awareness of her many gifts comes through repeatedly in her *Dialogue* as she writes of God who addresses her as "dearest daughter" and "beloved" and as she proclaims and exercises the mission entrusted to her. In the light of this abiding knowledge of God's "mad love" for her, Catherine was also able to acknowledge her radical finitude and her own sinful failures and she exhorted her followers and friends to do the same. She realized that detached from a deep experiential knowledge of God's love, self-knowledge can lead to despair or self-hatred, but she was confident that when self-knowledge is rooted in the depths of divine love, one can face one's limitations and admit to complicity in sin. That kind of self-awareness is essential if one is to speak the truth to others with compassion and without judgment. As God revealed to her in prayer:

> [Those who have clothed themselves in "gentle Truth"] find joy in everything. They do not sit in judgment on my servants or anyone else, but rejoice in every situation and every way of living they see, saying, "Thanks to you, eternal Father, that in your house there are so many dwelling places!"...In everything they find joy and the fragrance of the rose. This is true not only of good things; even when they see something that is clearly sinful they do not pass judgment, but rather feel a holy and genuine compassion, praying for the sinner and saying with perfect humility, "Today it is your turn; tomorrow it will be mine unless divine grace holds me up."[37]

Discernment requires not only speaking the truth, but also living in the truth of right relationship with the Creator and with all of creation. The struggle to live in right relationship requires the kind of patience that Catherine called the "marrow" of the tree of love. Only through patient attention can one come to discern "God's will" in the complexity of human, political, or ecclesial life. As Catherine discovered in her ecclesial and political attempts at mediation, a necessary aspect of the patience and perseverance required for authentic judgments of truth is the willingness to listen to, and pray for, those with whom we profoundly disagree. Since God's will cannot be identified with the will of any one person or group, the desire that God's will be done requires also learning to live with inner peace in situations of unresolved conflict even as one does what is possible to work toward just reconciliation and genuine peace. Catherine of Siena's mystical wisdom was honed throughout a lifetime in which her country was at war and the church was divided to the point of schism.

In her own challenging times, Catherine learned that discernment of truth is cultivated through prayer, patience, and perseverance. But as she was reminded early in her life, the clearest measure of one's authentic and rightly ordered love of God is to be found in love of others, specifically in the willingness to share their sorrows. As Catherine records God's words to her:

> I tell you, these beloved children of mine who have attained the highest perfection through perseverance and watching and constant humble prayer show that they love me in truth and that they have learned well by following this holy teaching of my Truth in their suffering and in the burdens they bear for their neighbors' salvation....[38]

The ability to make discerning judgments is thus inseparable from the compassionate heart fashioned in solidarity with those who suffer, just as Jesus' teaching was inseparable from the love that drove him to give his life for his friends. The more one's actions are motivated by love, the more clearly one can see "the light of truth." According to Catherine, true charity always carries the "lamp of holy discernment":

> Discernment is that light which dissolves all darkness, dissipates ignorance, and seasons every virtue and vir-

tuous deed. It has a prudence that cannot be deceived, a strength that is invincible, a constancy right up to the end, reaching as it does from heaven to earth, that is, from the knowledge of me to the knowledge of oneself, from love of me to love of one's neighbor.[39]

These insights of Catherine's into the difficult process of discerning the truth offer no concrete program for spiritual direction, for reconciliation within divided families, for consultation and decision-making in the church, for the way the magisterium should operate in dialogue with theologians, for how interreligious dialogue should proceed, or for how to decide where the Spirit is leading the church in terms of women's participation and ministries. However, her wisdom does point to the climate, attitudes, and conversion that are required for genuine discernment to proceed.

At its core, Catherine's understanding of discernment calls for unfailing commitment to truth. Precisely because the Spirit is the one who leads the community to see and embrace the Truth, the process of dialogue will involve the painful process of conversion that Bernard Lonergan has described as the self-correcting process of learning. As Lonergan described the constantly recurring process, new evidence or experience provokes new insights and understandings, which in turn require revised judgments that move us to new decisions and actions. The difficult part is that the process requires openness to conversion from the many forms of bias that block our ability to allow new experiences to challenge us or new evidence to prompt new insights, lest those new insights require revisions and even radical shifts in our thinking, judgments, and behavior.

The very possibility of that level of dialogue presumes that all participants will work to create and sustain a climate that fosters truth—precisely the climate that is so much in question not only in our society, but also in the church of our day. As a wide variety of loyal Catholics have argued, enforced silence, institutional denial, an authoritarian exercise of office, and punitive sanctions in areas of discussion that are crucial to the church's life, ministry, and integrity strain the credibility of the very claims to truth the church is hoping to defend.[40] In spite of Vatican II's proclamation that "the truth cannot impose itself except by virtue of its own truth as it makes its entrance into the individual at once quietly and with power" (*Dignitatis Humanae*, #1), we continue to witness severe sanctions for theological dissent, strict control of topics that are permissible for discussion even among bishops, new strains and even breakdowns in ecumenical and interreligious dialogue, denial or diminishment of calls for clerical and curial reform, and increasing polarization among those with differing views.

However, the responsibility of the breakdown in the climate of trust necessary for honest dialogue does not lie entirely with those in authority. In spite of their efforts to clarify the meaning of their stance, the Canadian bishops found themselves criticized by lay Catholics and the press for their support of a march opposing violence against women. Cardinal Bernardin was criticized not only by fellow cardinals, but also by lay Catholics and the media when he established the Common Ground initiative. The sociologist Katarina Schuth has identified the greatest challenge for faculty members in seminaries and theologates today to be "a climate of distrust and defensiveness," in which students publicly question the orthodoxy of professors and fellow students.[41] In spite of the growing polarization, however, bishops and theologians alike continue to speak and work for dialogue and mutual respect; the Common Ground initiative moves forward; faithful women hold fast to both their feminist and their Catholic loyalties and bring the two into creative dialogue; lay Catholic groups continue to organize grassroots meetings and exercise leadership in the broader church; gay and lesbian Catholics search for ways to claim both their religious and their sexual identities; religious leaders and theologians seek new openings for honest and fruitful ecumenical and interreligious dialogue; and respected church leaders remain voices for mediation, peace, and reconciliation in a world torn apart by violence.

The courage needed for genuine discernment involves not only the courage to listen, but also the courage to speak. When the climate in church or society does not welcome voices that differ, women and men with an authentic passion for the proclamation of truth need the courage and integrity required to speak the truth they see and to take the consequences for their speech. Catherine knew this well, having experienced at various points in her life the criticism and rejection of Pope Gregory XI, the Florentines, the people of Siena, her dear friend Raymond, many of the Dominican friars, many of her sisters in the Mantellate, and her own mother. She demanded no less courage from those she loved and advised. Thus she soundly criticized even Raymond for his failure to complete his mission from Urban VI to the King of France simply because he had heard that the enemy was lying in wait to kill him![42]

Even more painful than the criticism, resistance, and threats that arise from speaking challenging words to those outside the church is the suffering that can result from speaking one's perception of the truth within the church. Here again, Catherine's witness reminds us that love of the church and commitment to the truth are directly proportionate to one another. While her fierce loyalty to the church fueled her frank criticisms, at the same time she prayed fervently for those she criticized. She could not have imagined the twentieth-century language of a "sinful church," but she was keenly aware that the church was always in need of reform. She combined a remarkable realism about the church and its leaders with a deep faith that the mystical body of Christ was a far more profound reality than its institutional expressions. As Flannery O'Connor once expressed it: "I think that the church is the only thing that is going to make the terrible world we are coming to endurable; the only thing that makes the church endurable is that it is somehow the body of Christ and that on this we are fed."[43]

Catherine's love of a broken world and church led to the deepest source of her wisdom—her share in the wisdom of the cross. What Catherine described as her entry into the side of Christ crucified was for her a share in God's own compassion, a participation in the Spirit's gift of mercy. In the final chapter we explore how this wisdom of compassion gave authority to her prophetic words.

Three

The Authority of Compassion

In the end, Catherine of Siena's sense of authority and the wisdom of her words are inseparable from her understanding of the Christian life as participation in the redemptive suffering of Jesus Christ. Her passionate speech emerged from her passion for God and her share in the passion of Jesus Christ. Yet an initial reading of Catherine's own desire, and her advice to others, to be bathed and even drowned in the blood of Jesus, to drink from the wounds of Christ, to remain fastened to the cross, to feed at the table of the cross, to be a servant and slave of the servants of Christ Jesus, and to embrace martyrdom, may lead to the conclusion that Catherine's spirituality of the cross is not only a distant mirror, but a radically distorted one that has little to offer to women today.

There are, without doubt, aspects of Catherine's life and spirituality that cannot and should not be retrieved in our day. In a time when eating disorders threaten the lives and health of countless young women, Catherine's radical asceticism, named by Rudoph Bell as "holy anorexia," cannot be endorsed as a contemporary path to holiness. Nevertheless, Caroline Walker Bynum's treatment of the religious significance of food and fasting for medieval women can help us see that control over food was one way that Catherine and other medieval women exercised both autonomy and authority and suggests some intriguing insights about women's eucharistic spirituality then and now.[1] While Catherine's eucharistic spirituality cannot be uncritically appropriated, her insights into the Eucharist as nursing at the breast of Christ, the connection she drew between participation in the Eucharist and solidarity with a suffering world ("entering the wounds of Christ"), and her longing for the

Eucharist even when clerical control over the sacraments was exercised by ministers of whom she was rightly critical, all offer challenges and possibilities for contemporary women's rethinking of eucharistic spirituality. We are quite rightly repulsed to learn that Catherine drank the pus from the cancerous wound of a dying woman who was herself critical of Catherine, but whom Catherine continued to nurse during the plague. But what can we learn from this sign of the depth of her commitment to remain in solidarity with the suffering other?

Catherine's language of servanthood and slavery can seem to glorify systems in which women were expected to be servants whether in family, church, or society. Likewise, it can appear to legitimate the ways in which white women of the dominant class have participated in the oppression of women of color who were their servants or slaves, or the ways in which poverty continues to force women into multiple forms of servitude, including sexual exploitation.[2] Retrieving the centrality of an authentic understanding of Christian service requires attending not only to gender, but to the interrelated dynamics of multiple forms of oppression, and calls us to reflect on how the specifics of the call to conversion differ widely according to one's concrete situation in life. While Catherine in her day did not attend to social or political analysis in her entreaties to those to whom she wrote to take up their cross, her letters show that she was keenly aware that what conversion meant for each person was unique and required genuine discernment. As we appropriate her insights in our day, we do so aware that what it meant for Catherine and the popes, queens and kings, abbesses, clerics, or political leaders of her day to become "servants of the servants of God" is considerably different from the challenges facing a woman caught in a web of economic, racial, ethnic, and political oppression today.

The growth of violence in our homes, cities, and world— especially the violence perpetrated in the name of God or religion—quite rightly raises cautions about a spirituality of the cross that could be used to legitimate radical suffering as "God's will," or to reinforce the perception that Christianity exhorts masochism. But to read Catherine of Siena's writings through those lenses is to fail to see both her own passionate resistance to suffering and evil and the root metaphors in her testimony to the God who is "mad with love" for creation and who has "kneaded together humanity and divinity" in the incarnation.

Nevertheless, our world and church are not those of Catherine's fourteenth-century Italy; nor can our piety and theology be hers. We live at the beginning of the third millennium with violence on the rise around the globe, where some of the most fierce and devastating terrors are wrought with the fervor of religious conviction. We live in an age of religious intolerance and the straining, if not the breakdown, of religious dialogue in the name of truth. Catherine's convictions that salvation can be found only in conversion to Christianity, her imagery of the cross as weapon of defense, the anti-Judaism in her writings, her advocacy of the Crusades—all are aspects of her theology that can no longer be reconciled with the God of mercy who created humanity in all of its diversity for union with God and with all of creation. Catherine was keenly aware of the power of sin as the cause of so much of the world's suffering, but her focus was not on the question of why a good God would allow the suffering of the innocent that so haunts those who struggle to believe today. While Catherine's emphasis on the passion and death of Jesus is striking, a corresponding development of the power of the resurrection is lacking. The acceptance of suffering and material poverty as "God's will," which Catherine advocated, can lead to a legitimation of evils that are of human origin and give rise to an image of God and a spirituality that are destructive and dangerous for women and for all those who suffer injustice and violence. Likewise, Catherine's acceptance of inherited notions such as Augustine's view of original sin as pride, and Eve's responsibility for having led Adam into sin, as well as some of her language of self-abasement and body-soul dualism, are all problematic for women who have internalized a fundamental lack of self-worth. For these women a genuine journey of conversion requires the struggle to realize their goodness and dignity and the sacredness of their bodies and sexuality.

In spite of these reservations, the wager here is that the fourteenth-century mirror of Catherine's life and writings can cast light on our own attempts to embrace a spirituality that respects the human dignity of all women, men, and children; that inspires us to stay in the struggle to overcome oppression of all kinds, whether based on gender, sexual orientation, race, or class; and that is rooted in the freedom, joy, and contemplative intimacy with God that sustained Catherine throughout her life.

We will look first at Catherine's frequent exhortations in her letters to embrace the cross, and then at the multiple metaphors for salvation or redemption that are found in the *Dialogue* and Catherine's prayers. While Catherine does not attempt to systematize into a single theology of redemption the diverse images and metaphors drawn from scripture, liturgy, and mystical experience that appear in her writings, central themes do recur. These leitmotifs of her thought can offer guidance in deciphering why Catherine consistently connected her authority with the authority of the blood of Jesus or Christ crucified. Finally, with an eye toward the differences between the theological challenges of Catherine's century and our own, we will return to the question of whether Catherine's approach to the authority of the crucified One can help us to see how the authority of women's speech about God today remains fundamentally tied to the authority of compassion.

Catherine's Exhortations to Embrace the Cross

For Catherine the preacher, as for the apostle Paul, it is Christ crucified who is "the power of God and the wisdom of

God" (1 Cor 1:24). This is perhaps most evident in Catherine's letters where she uses the symbol of the blood of Christ in all but six of her almost four hundred individually-tailored "sermons" addressed to the needs of very different persons. Almost every letter begins with a salutation that rooted Catherine's wisdom in the wisdom of the cross. Typically, she established the authority of her message with greetings such as: "In the name of Jesus Christ crucified and of gentle Mary" and continued: "I, Catherine, servant and slave of the servants of Jesus Christ, write to you in his precious blood...."

Catherine repeatedly turned to the wisdom of the cross in offering advice in diverse situations. To an elderly widow living a frivolous and superficial life, Catherine wrote: "Did our relatives or friends or anyone else redeem us? No, Christ crucified alone was the Lamb who with unfathomable love offered his body to be sacrificed, giving us himself as bath and medicine, food and clothing, and as a bed in which we can rest."[3] For this woman to embrace the cross in her life meant to develop the appropriate asceticism and focus that would enable her to reorder her life with God at the center. Catherine reminded another lay woman who belonged to the Mantellate, "We ought to be servants because we are bought with his blood,"[4] advising her companion to direct her gratitude and love for God into service of her neighbor. To her own first spiritual director, a Dominican friar who was also her cousin, Catherine appealed, "I beg you to remain fastened and nailed to the cross," describing it as her desire that he be "united to and transformed into God" and signing her letter "Catherine, servant and slave redeemed with the blood of the Son of God...." The intent of her exhortation becomes more apparent when one realizes that Catherine consistently insisted that Jesus' obedience unto death was a perseverance in love so that he was held to the cross only by "nails of love."[5]

In other letters to her family and friends, Catherine drew out other dimensions of the wisdom of the cross to respond to

their concrete dilemmas. When her brother was in financial dif-
ficulty, she begged him "to bear all your troubles patiently," to
reflect on the brevity of life, and "to consider that we can gain
benefit even from our troubles."[6] Catherine advised her niece, a
contemplative nun who was experiencing difficulties in prayer,
that the one who is faithful to prayer sees clearly that Christ "ran
to the shameful death on the cross in obedience to the Father
and for our salvation....Bathe and drown yourself in the gentle
blood of your bridegroom."[7] The broader context of Catherine's
writings again makes clear that Christ's running to embrace
death was the race of one who was "mad with love" and filled
with "hunger for our salvation." Catherine was convinced that
the blood of Jesus, as that affection of the God who is a "crazy
lover," was the bond of all deep friendship and authentic love.
Thus she begged Raymond to

> pray earnestly that you and I together may drown our-
> selves in the blood of the humble Lamb. This will
> make us strong and faithful. We shall then feel the fire
> of divine love…just as our love for all people in gen-
> eral corresponds to a general faith, so a particular faith
> operates between those who love each other more
> closely, as you and I do.[8]

But when another friend, the Augustinian William Flete, refused to respond to Urban's request to come to Rome, for fear
that he would lose the peace and tranquility of his contemplative hermitage in the political and ecclesiastical struggles in
Rome, Catherine was firm in reminding him that love of God
is inseparable from the love of neighbor that he was resisting.
She was forthright in her challenge that following Christ
requires sacrifice for the sake of the neighbor—or in this
case, the church—in need. She challenged her friend and his
companion:

> I Catherina, servant and slave of the servants of Jesus
> Christ, am writing to you in his precious blood....I
> long to see you so losing yourselves that you will seek
> no peace or quiet except in Christ crucified. I long to
> see you at the table of the cross, conceiving hunger
> for God's honor, the salvation of souls, and the reform
> of holy church. We see the church in such great need
> today that it is imperative for you to forget yourselves
> and come out of your woods to help her....If you
> don't, you will be out of tune with God's will.[9]

Catherine's political and ecclesiastical interventions likewise centered on the teachings of Christ that were to be learned
at the "table of the cross." When the authorities in Bologna were
placing heavy burdens on the poor and appointing other officials on the basis of partisanship, prejudice, and bribery, Catherine
called for their conversion as a participation in the kenosis or
self-emptying of Jesus. She exhorted them to give up their fear
of losing status and to embrace their responsibilities to rule for
the common good with justice tempered by mercy: "That is why
I told you that I desired to see you divested of the old self and
clothed with the new self, Christ crucified."[10] When Pope
Gregory XI feared returning to Rome because of rumors that he
would be murdered, Catherine insisted that he hold fast to his
resolution to return, following the example of Christ crucified.
In the context of the wars between the Italian city-states, she
reminded him that the only weapon he should rely on was the
cross. Here, her allusion to the cross as weapon clearly refers to
its spiritual power to inspire courage and perseverance:

> ...dearest father, follow him whose vicar you are,
> deliberating and deciding for yourself, and saying in
> the presence of all who oppose you: "Even if I should
> lose my life a thousand times, I want to do the will of

my eternal Father."...So, have courage, and don't be unnecessarily afraid. Take up the weapon of the most holy cross which is security and life for Christians. Let those who want to, say whatever they like: you hold firmly to your holy resolution.[11]

In spite of all of his limitations, Catherine supported Gregory's successor, Urban VI, in his efforts at church reform, but she objected to the arrogant and harsh manner in which he alienated the very people he was sent to serve. Again, she turned to the crucified One, this time as model of mercy:

I beg and urge you for the love of Christ crucified, and out of love for that blood of which you are the minister, not to delay in welcoming back mercifully those sheep who have left the fold [the Tuscan cities who had rebelled against the Pope]....Soften their obduracy with kindness and holiness, offering them the benefit of belonging to the fold once more....Be content to take from the sick only as much as they can give....[12]

In perhaps her best-known and most controversial letter, Catherine wrote to Raymond about how she counseled the political prisoner, Niccolò di Toldo, to face his execution with courage and steadfast faith. She relates to Raymond how on the day of Niccolò's execution, after he joined her at Eucharist and received holy communion for the first time, she urged Niccolò: "Courage, my dear brother; we shall soon be at the wedding feast. You will go there bathed in the sweet blood of God's Son, and in the sweet name of Jesus." At the time of the execution, as Catherine narrates the story, she saw Christ standing ready to receive Niccolò's blood into his own. She describes thus her vision of Niccolò's welcome into infinite mercy and crucified love:

94

After [Christ] received the blood and the desire, he received the soul also, and plunged it into the store-house of his open side brimming with mercy....When he was received in this way by our powerful God (who has the power to do it), the Son who is wisdom and incarnate Word gave him a share in the crucified love with which, in obedience to the Father, he himself bore his own painful and shameful death for the sake of all humanity, and the hands of the holy Spirit sealed him within.[13]

After the execution Catherine explains that she could not remove the prisoner's blood, which had splashed on her, because she was so aware of its fragrance, and records her great envy in seeing herself left behind.

Catherine's Metaphors for Redemption

Like her letters, Catherine's prayers and the *Dialogue* present multiple images of the cross and encompass diverse theological perspectives on what it means to be saved or redeemed in and through the blood of Jesus. Although Catherine does allude to the earliest Christian struggle with the scandal of the cross in references to the shameful death of Jesus, her reflections do not begin from below with the life and ministry of Jesus that led to his execution—as do most contemporary Christologies. Rather, the starting point for her meditations and prayers is from above; she begins with the post-resurrection faith claims made throughout the Christian tradition about what God has done for the salvation of the world in and through Jesus. Catherine draws on and incorporates a number of the classic metaphors for redemption. She alludes to Christ as paying the price to redeem sinners from the bondage of sin, healing their wounds and washing them clean in his blood, reconciling alienated humankind to friendship with God, making satisfaction and restoring God's honor, atoning for sins, unlocking the gates of the garden of heaven with the key of his obedience, bringing about a new creation, and transforming humankind. In particular, given her own ministry of reconciliation and peacemaking, Catherine saw the social effects of sin in hatred, violence, and war and emphasized Christ's role as reconciler:

> And you, Jesus Christ,
> our reconciler,
> our refashioner,
> our redeemer—
> you, Word and love,
> were made our mediator.
> You turned our great war with God into a great
>   peace.[14]

But Catherine did not view salvation primarily as a remedy for sin; rather, she stresses that humankind and all of creation were destined in love from the beginning. Drawing on a favorite motif from the Eastern tradition that was also present, if not emphasized as heavily, in Augustine's writings, Catherine highlights the saving grace of the incarnation. To use her bread-baking imagery, divinity was "kneaded into" humanity in the incarnation. As Catherine marveled over the call of humankind to participate in the very life of God, she prayed: "you, God, became human and humanity became God."[15] She stressed that the motive for the incarnation was fundamentally love: "you, high eternal Trinity, acted as if you were drunk with love, infatuated with your creature."[16]

That same boundless "immeasurable love" is at the heart of Catherine's imagery for redemption from sin. Thus she describes not only the cross, but also the incarnation, as redemptive:

When you saw that this tree could bear no fruit
but the fruit of death
because it was cut off from you who are life,
you came to its rescue
with the same love
with which you had created it:
you engrafted your divinity
into the dead tree of our humanity.
O sweet tender engrafting![17]

Accenting the motif of God as lover in her *Dialogue*, Catherine writes of the death of Jesus and the descent into hell as demonstrating the extent to which divine love will go to be united with humanity: "O mad lover! It was not enough for you to take on our humanity: You had to die as well! Nor was death enough: You descended to the depths to summon our holy ancestors and fulfill your truth and mercy in them."[18] Catherine refers as well to Christ as the "mad lover" who ran eagerly to his death, the one who "by being stretched out on the cross...embraced us."[19]

Some of the metaphors for redemption that Catherine inherited and used have proved problematic in recent times, both in terms of the image of God they disclose and in terms of the spiritualities they have spawned, perpetuating at times either masochism or religious violence or both. Within her texts are references to the cross as the Son's fulfillment of an "obedience that his Father had laid on him"; to Christ's humanity as "the bait by which God caught the devil"; to God's choice to "punish your [God's] own natural Son for the sin of your adopted child"; to the Father willing "that the Son's feet might be nailed, but so his body might be a staircase for you."

At the same time, to read those texts out of context is to miss what for Catherine was central: the blood of Jesus—which was the life-force by which he lived—was love freely poured out; the obedience of Christ to which we are called is the obedience of love; the punishment Christ endured was the result of human sin, not God's will for Jesus, or for any human being. Hence Catherine can address God as "O unutterable mercy" in the same prayer in which she speaks of the punishment for sin which Christ bore (Prayer 23). In her understanding, the final gift of love that was involved in Jesus' handing over of his life was the very life of God poured out for the sake of humanity. In her *Dialogue*, she offers the following interpretation of how the cross reveals God's love:

> I let them open his side so that you might see his inmost heart. I set him like an open hostelry where you could see and taste my unspeakable love for you when you found and saw my divinity united with your humanity....I have made the blood to be a bath to wash away your sins....[20]

The blood that Catherine exhorts her readers to bathe, drink, and drown in is the cup of charity, forgiveness, and compassion. To share in that cup is to constantly expand the scope of those who are included in one's concern, just as God invited Catherine to "keep expanding your heart and your affection in the immeasurable greatness of my mercy."[21]

Catherine's classic images for redemption as atonement, satisfaction, and payment of a debt owed to God are familiar metaphors that have functioned in often quite literal and univocal ways in the Christian imagination. But what has received less attention in ecclesial celebrations of Catherine's gift of wisdom are the female metaphors for salvation that were also central to Catherine's prayer and writings. Like many medieval writers, she regularly used female images in developing her understanding of how human beings share in salvation, particularly in her central metaphor of the saving blood that we are invited to eat and drink.

In the tradition of her day, Christ's blood was most often used as a symbol for the washing away of sin, a symbol she also incorporates. However, Catherine's emphasis was on blood as food or life.[22] In the *Dialogue* she speaks of God inviting her to drink from the breast of divine charity, and she encourages her followers to do the same. The Holy Spirit is pictured as mother who nurses the soul at the breast of divine charity. Christ is our "wet-nurse" who drank the bitter medicine of his painful death on the cross "so that he might heal and give life to you who were babies weakened by sin."[23] Catherine's letters, too, include multiple images of drinking at the breast of Christ. This image would have had particular significance for Catherine based on her own experience. To drink at the breast of Christ crucified is to taste the high eternal Godhead and to drink in God's blessings.[24] As Bynum has demonstrated, in Catherine's era breast milk was considered to be blood—the essential source of life could be provided only by female bodies.[25]

The eucharistic connections here are unmistakable—just as mothers feed their children from their own bodies, so God nourishes us with her divine milk of charity. Only those who eat and drink from the divine breast will live: "[Whoever] feeds on my flesh and drinks my blood remains in me, and I in [them]" (John 6:57). Catherine's great respect for the clergy derived from their authority over the sacraments, an authority she never questioned. In that context, it is particularly noteworthy that she imaged both Christ and the Holy Spirit as female and eucharistic feeding as a maternal activity. Further, on one occasion on which Catherine was deprived of Eucharist in spite of her great longing for it, she was fed by Christ directly, to the astonishment of the eucharistic presider.[26]

Catherine's food imagery for salvation extends to another metaphor drawn from the traditionally female role of preparing the table and feeding the family, a role she shared in her own ministry among the poor. Catherine envisions the Trinity as both feeding us and deepening our hunger for the salvation of others (intensifying our desire to "eat souls"). At the "table of the cross" God's children are nourished by Christ's teaching, enjoy the taste of the milk of charity, "grow fat" on true and solid virtues, and "eat the food of souls" by learning to bear with their neighbors and to support them.[27] In Catherine's imagery, God, too, "hungers" for the salvation of souls and the cross serves as a table of "holy desire," since Christ hungered for the redemption of humanity.

Closely related to Catherine's imagery of drinking from the breast of Christ, and often used interchangeably, is her image of immersing oneself in the wounds of Christ crucified. Catherine emphasized that even beyond the resurrection Christ still bears his wounds and scars, which are the wounds of humanity taken into the very heart of God. In the radical solidarity with the wounded world that his scars symbolize, Christ continues to cry out for mercy.[28] In his version of Catherine's life, Raymond describes Catherine's experience of feeling mystically drawn to drink from the wound in Jesus' side, which she identifies with both his heart and his breast. Just as love of God and love of neighbor were inseparable for Catherine, so too was plunging oneself into the side of Jesus inseparable from embracing the suffering of the world. Convinced that human suffering for the sake of the neighbor was a genuine participation in the sufferings of Christ, Catherine was equally persuaded that we are called to "pressure God with our tears." God's plan for the mystic body of holy church is that we be converted and saved through one another.[29] Just as in tears of fire the Holy Spirit weeps with love and longing for the well-being of the world, we too are called to participate in the "lover's lament" of God's own mercy and sorrow through love of neighbor.

Can Women Claim the Cross Today?

Catherine of Siena's authority—the power of her words, her life, and her witness—was rooted deeply in her experience of what it meant to participate in the redemptive suffering of Jesus Christ. Her eucharistic spirituality, her solidarity with the poor and the suffering of Siena, her political engagement, her calls for the reform of the church and especially its ministers, and her life of contemplative prayer were all interwoven strands of her experience of life as a share in the paschal mystery. In our day women continue to experience their lives as a mysterious participation in a larger web of life, death, and new life. Many, however, even among those who were baptized into the body of Christ, no longer identify or experience their passion for life and their share in suffering as a participation in the death and resurrection of Jesus. There are some who long for a spirituality that can connect their life journeys and their experience of loss and dying with hope for new life, promise of reunions beyond death, and renewed energy to stay involved in the struggle for justice. But they often fail to find those resources in their churches or liturgies or in the symbol of Christ crucified. Still other women do speak with passion about finding the deepest grounding of their lives and energy in identifying their struggles and joys with the life, death, and resurrection of Jesus.

Attending to such diverse voices can help to clarify what really is redemptive in the paschal mystery of Jesus' life, death, and resurrection. In contrast to the spirituality in which many women have been schooled, it is not suffering or death that is redemptive. Even the death of Jesus is salvific only in the context of his life and resurrection. As the apostle Paul reminds us: "If Christ was not raised, your faith is worthless" (1 Cor 15:17). It was not suffering that saved us, but rather a love that was fierce enough to triumph over the forces of death and evil and a compassion that was broad enough to encompass all of creation.

101

Likewise, the authority of women's voices and lives is rooted not in their experiences of suffering, but in the passion with which they have resisted or endured suffering and the compassion that they embody.

Why has the symbol of the cross, so much at the heart of Catherine's spirituality and authority, become so problematic in contemporary Christian theology, especially among women? Two reasons stand out. First, Christian theology, piety, and pastoral practice over the centuries exalted the cross as symbol of God's victory over evil and sin, while losing sight of the most fundamental scandal that haunted the first Christians: in and of itself, the cross was a weapon of execution, a form of capital punishment. Considered from the viewpoint of history, Jesus was an innocent man who was unjustly executed. Betrayed by one of his own disciples, abandoned by many of his closest friends, handed over to the Roman Empire by religious authorities, sentenced by a political leader who knew him to be innocent, he was shamed, mocked, and tortured by soldiers, and executed as a criminal, dying on a cross between two thieves.

A second scandal in the tradition results from the way teachers, pastoral counselors, or preachers, have urged women, the poor, and those who have suffered a variety of forms of discrimination and violence, toward passivity. Using biblical language, but distorting the gospel message, those who were recognized authorities in the tradition have exhorted those who were victims of violence to bear their cross, to turn the other cheek, and to offer up their suffering as a share in the sufferings of Jesus Christ, rather than to resist evil, to break the silence, and to end cycles of violence. Early on in the development of the feminist critique of how the Christian tradition functioned for women, Mary Daly identified the scapegoat syndrome that encouraged women disciples to accept the role of passive victim.[30] That critique has been echoed by many women and feminist theologians, reaching a new level of urgency in the context of the documented growth of domestic abuse and violence against women and children around the world. Contemporary as well as traditional theologies of the cross that speak of God willing the death of his [sic] only son and that justify the suffering and death of Jesus in terms of the Father's gift of his beloved child for us and for our salvation have been roundly rejected by feminist theologians as "a form of cosmic child abuse."[31] Womanist theologian Delores Williams, reflecting from the perspective of black women who have been expected and even forced to perform multiple surrogacy roles throughout a history of exploitation, has argued that as Jesus' ministry and resurrection reveal, Jesus came for life, not for death. According to Williams, "There is nothing divine in the blood of the cross....[To glorify the cross] is to glorify suffering and to render [black women's] exploitation sacred."[32] While these arguments are often countered by the charge that the cross is fundamentally a symbol of Jesus' self-giving love, Elisabeth Schüssler Fiorenza has remarked that that theology is even more problematic than theologies of the cross that emphasize Jesus' obedience unto death, because they offer a psychological and religious warrant for the exploitation of women in the name of love and self-sacrifice.[33]

No contemporary theology of the cross can avoid addressing how the cross has functioned to foster violence and injustice against women, as well as to develop passivity and a false understanding of self-sacrificial love among women. But women from around the world who recognize and oppose those false appropriations of the cross have raised their voices to speak of their own experiences of finding courage and sustaining power in identifying their struggles against the forces of death with the passion and death of Jesus. They know and proclaim from their experience—as did Catherine—that a passion for life and a passion for justice are intimately connected. They also know from experience what it means to endure the passion in maintaining integrity, fidelity, and love in a world of sin.

Voices of Passion and Resistance

Womanist scholars are well aware of how the misuse of the cross has contributed to the exploitation of black women. Yet some have argued that in their response to situations of radical injustice, those same women have redeemed the symbol of the cross by identifying their courage, resistance, ability to survive, and strength to nourish others with their faith in Jesus. Thus Shawn Copeland notes how in slave narratives written by women (as distinct from the way female slaves were interpreted by men), women describe themselves not as passive subjects, but as active agents who make whatever decisions are possible to take charge of their lives and to resist brutality. These women who held no authority or power in any dominant system nevertheless spoke with authority in creating their own language— the language of sass. In speaking back and speaking up and claiming their own voices, Copeland notes they used sass "to guard, regain, and secure self-esteem; to obtain and hold psychological distance; to speak truth; to challenge the 'atmosphere of moral ambiguity that surrounds them,' and sometimes, to protect against sexual assault."[34]

In the words of their masters, the cross was a symbol of submission, but in their own words, "[the enslaved Africans] sang because they saw the result of the cross—triumph over the principalities and powers of death, triumph over evil in this world."[35] These women redeemed the cross from its misuse and abuse by forging their own testimonies of survival and resistance and identifying their struggles to resist evil with the symbol of the cross as God's power to defeat evil. The hope that emerged from that struggle enabled them to pass on to their children memories of a God who liberated slaves, stories of the courage and resistance of their mothers and grandmothers, and hope for a promised land and freedom. Surviving their own experiences of suffering, they handed on to their children not only resources for survival and resistance, but also the ability to transform suffering into active participation in God's redeeming of the world. Recognizing that the suffering imposed upon them was a violation of their God-given dignity and an outrage to God, they gave meaning and dignity to the struggle to live and to pass on life in the face of the forces of death.

Asian women who have been active in struggles for liberation have also claimed the power they have experienced in identifying with the passion of Jesus. Reflecting on the experience of Filipino women who have been arrested, raped, tortured, imprisoned, and sometimes murdered, Lydia Lascano names the experience of these political martyrs as going beyond keeping vigil at the foot of the cross: "Today many Filipino women do not merely accompany Christ to Calvary as spectators. They carry the cross with him and undergo his passion in an act of identification with his suffering."[36] But Lascano makes it clear that this identification with the suffering Christ cannot be separated from the active resistance to evil which led to the deaths of Filipino women. Remembering their stories empowers other women to see the structural causes of the sufferings they endure and to join their voices and lives in movements for justice, liberation, and peace. The authority of the voices of the women who have gone before them arises from the integrity of their lives and their radical courage in the face of evil, even unto death.

When Asian women gathered in Mexico in 1986 with an intercontinental group of women theologians from geographical areas and groups marked by poverty and multiple oppressions, they confirmed how central the mysteries of the passion and the cross are in the faith of the people of their diverse countries. Yet they hastened to add that the whole point of Jesus' suffering was new life. They clearly distinguished forms of suffering that are demonic and destructive from the participation in suffering that can be redemptive.

Suffering that is inflicted by the oppressor and is pas-
sively accepted does not lead to life; it is destructive and
demonic....But suffering that is part of the struggle for
the sake of God's reign or that results from the uncon-
trollable and mysterious conditions of humankind is
redeeming and is rooted in the Paschal Mystery,
evocative of the rhythm of pregnancy, delivery, and
birth. This kind of suffering is familiar to women of all
times, who participate in the pains of birth and the
joys of new creation.[37]

December 2010 marks the thirtieth anniversary of the murders of four North American church women who also knew well
the distinction between the evil of suffering that resulted from
injustice inflicted on a people and the possibility that active participation in suffering in solidarity with others can be redemptive. Maura Clarke, Ita Ford, Dorothy Kazel, and Jean Donovan,
the four North American church women, threw in their lot with
the crucified people of El Salvador and shared the lot of the one
for whom their country is named. In a retreat journal, Maura
Clarke revealed something of her own theology of the cross
after learning of the death of the leaders of the liberation movement and the disappearance of over 350 *campesinos* in the area
where she had ministered in Nicaragua. She wrote: "I saw the
tortured people who fight for justice today in the place of
Christ, and I pictured the rulers and the military as the high
priests. I envisioned the poor, Ricardo, Asuncion, Dionisio, as
the tortured Jesus."[38] These women embraced solidarity with the
poor not out of any sort of glorification or romanticization of
suffering, but because it was among the poor of the world that
they discovered the good news of the reign of God at work in
the world despite all the evidence to the contrary. In contem-
plating her own decision to go to El Salvador, Ita Ford wrote of

her experience of paschal mystery and what it would mean to live in solidarity with those who are powerless:

> The challenge that we live daily is to enter into the paschal mystery with faith. Am I willing to suffer with the people here, the suffering of the powerless? Can I say to my neighbors, "I have no solution to this situation; I don't know the answers, but I will walk with you, search with you, be with you?"[39]

Lay missioner Jean Donovan, too, wrote of the children who held her to her commitment to walk with them in spite of the impending danger to all who were identified with the church's stand against the injustice and violence in El Salvador. Two weeks before her death she wrote to a friend of how her own heart was being stretched by their pain:

> Several times I have decided to leave El Salvador. I almost could except for the children, the poor, bruised victims of this insanity. Who would care for them? Whose heart could be so staunch as to favour the reasonable thing in a sea of their tears and loneliness? Not mine, dear friend, not mine.[40]

The words and lives of these faithful women offer a contemporary version of the power that Catherine of Siena identified as entering into the wounds of Jesus, of bathing in and drinking the blood of Jesus. None of these witnesses sought or embraced death; on the contrary, they protested the injustice and sin that caused the spilling of the blood of untold numbers of the poor on a daily basis. They spoke honestly of their own fears of death and torture, of their loneliness, of the frustration of their efforts on behalf of life, justice, and peace. But the suffering and death they encountered in their fidelity to the God of life and their solidarity with the powerless and the little ones, now form an integral part of the witness they continue to bear. Particularly for many North Americans who previously resisted seeing any complicity between our country's economic, political, and military policies and the fate of the poor in Latin America, the blood of these martyrs was indeed the seed of conversion. The authority of the witness of their lives was strong enough to move the United States ambassador to El Salvador to challenge publicly United States policy in that country and to continue to inspire protests and political action such as the annual demonstration to close the School of the Americas in Fort Benning, Georgia.

In the words and lives of the medieval mystic who longed for martyrdom and her contemporary sisters who dreaded it, but who faced that possibility with courage, it becomes clear that the biblical symbol of blood is fundamentally a sign of life, not death. Blood is the most basic source of life that sustains us. The martyrs of El Salvador poured out their blood in sharing the daily lives of their people—not only in the moment of death. They mourned and protested the loss of life of the unnamed and unremembered poor in their blood-stained country. In the end their blood too shared in the redemptive power of the blood of Christ crucified—the blood of the innocent that cries to heaven for justice and vindication. What Oscar Romero, the Archbishop of San Salvador who had been assassinated by the military eight months earlier as he celebrated Eucharist in a convent chapel, professed shortly before his own death was true of them as well:

> My life has been threatened many times. I have to confess that as a Christian, I don't believe in death without resurrection. If they kill me, I will rise again in the Salvadoran people. If they should go so far as to carry out their threats, I want you to know that I now offer my blood to God for justice and the resurrection of El Salvador. Martyrdom is a grace of God that I do not feel

worthy of. But if God accepts the sacrifice of my life, my hope is that my blood will be like a seed of liberty and a sign that our hopes will soon become reality.[41]

Romero did not always speak with such passion; neither did the women of El Salvador initially see themselves as called to speak in public rallies and to call their country to repentance and conversion. Rather, their words emerged from their love of people and their land and from their pain and outrage at seeing them devastated and destroyed. For Romero, the turning point in his conversion was the murder of a respected Jesuit priest, Rutilio Grande, along with an old man, and a young boy. For Jean Donovan, it was the children who kept her in El Salvador even unto death. The specific relationships and circumstances differ, but in each of those cases a passion for life and relationship gave birth to voices of protest and lives of courage. In the lives of each of the witnesses named here and of countless others who gave their lives in the struggle for justice, a share in God's own heart stretched the human heart to the point where both women and men chose to lay down their lives for their friends.

Negative Contrast Experience and the Politics of Compassion

In each of those situations, an experience of radical and dehumanizing suffering gave rise to words spoken with authority and passion, sometimes unto death. Children and young people, such as the school children who led the protest in Soweto or Ruby Bridges and Melba Pattillo Beals who were among the first to integrate public schools in the southern United States, have risked their lives to protest racism and other systemic violations of human rights. In those and other profiles

in courage, women, men, and children found they could no
longer be silent in the face of events that violate human dignity
and the integrity of creation. In those fundamental experiences
of injustice or radical human suffering that Edward Schillebeeckx
has called "negative contrast experiences," one can only cry out
in protest: "This cannot go on." Betty Williams, the founder of
the Center of Peace in Northern Ireland, describes from experience how powerful words emerge from that kind of pain:

> I gave a voice to something that the women of Ireland
> were feeling at the time. They were sick of losing their
> husbands, sons and daughters. They were in enor-
> mous pain. I think probably when I yelled for peace—
> because that's what I really did, you know—that the
> women responded in kind. I couldn't really say that
> Betty Williams started the peace movement in Ireland
> because that would be another lie. The death of three
> children started the peace movement in Ireland. Betty
> Williams was just the voice—yelling out for them.[42]

Sometimes the words of protest are the only words we can
speak clearly in the face of complex forces of evil woven into
the fabric of our lives and world. We cannot always see or name
the way forward. Further, no liberation front or political or
social program can be identified with the reign of God. But even
the cry of protest is a word of grace that moves us to resistance
and to searching for another way. The beginning of finding a
new path is speaking the truth of what clearly is not God's will
for human life or for the church. But for experiences of negativ-
ity to be ones of contrast, rather than mere confirmation of life's
absurdity and harshness, one must have had at least fragmentary
moments of meaning, love, and joy. It is precisely the life and
love we have known, the compassion of God we have tasted,
that prompts us to say that life could be different, that peace is

possible, that relationships can be mended. Likewise, it is the experience and promise of a welcoming community, a shared table, and the unconditional forgiveness of God, that sustains our commitment to become more fully the body of Christ and to call the body as a whole to be more of a sacrament of salvation in our world. Our hopes are shaped by the stories and rituals that form the horizons of our imaginations.

Catherine of Siena's image of what was possible for Italy, for the church, for the persons she loved and counseled, and for herself was nurtured by her experience of the God she heard proclaimed from the scriptures, celebrated in liturgy, and tasted in mystical prayer. The God who was mad with love for creation, the God who became our bridge of reconciliation so we would not drown in life's hard times, the God who waits on us at table and nurses us at her breast, was a God whose will is always for fuller life. Thus, whether addressing the war of the Italian city-states, the schism in the church, the interdict that deprived the Florentines of a viable economic life as well as of the sacraments, the corruption of the clergy, political persecution, the lies and gossip that destroyed a relationship or community, or an individual's lack of trust in God's mercy or providence, Catherine's words reflected her conviction: this cannot go on. She may have exercised the rhetorical flourish of asking her hearers to "pardon my boldness," but that never stopped her from speaking when she saw an injustice or another person in pain. And she clearly intended that her calls for conversion would lead to action and change—whether from political rulers, popes, or her own mother.

But Catherine of Siena's appeals for conversion and reform did not include calls for the kind of structural reform of society and church that we now realize are necessary to sustain and empower right relationships. Still, her basic gospel insight that love of God and love of neighbor are the same love is at the heart of the kind of "political holiness" that is called for today.[43]

Catherine who longed for the contemplative life of her room discovered that prayer pushed her to the streets and into the arena
of politics, and her encounters there sent her to God begging for
mercy and assistance. Crucial to Catherine's experience of the
unity of love of God and love of neighbor is her insight that this
is not a matter of love of God spilling over into love of neighbor, but the two are in fact one single love. In a passage in her
Dialogue she writes with authority of God's words to her on this:

> I ask you to love me with the same love with which I
> love you. But for me you cannot do this, for I loved
> you without being loved….This is why I have given
> you your neighbors as intermediary: so that you can
> do for them what you cannot do for me—that is love
> them without any concern for thanks and without
> looking for any profit for yourself. And whatever you
> do for them I will consider done for me….You should
> love your neighbors with the same love with which
> you love me.[44]

In our world of global communication, international politics, and economies dominated by multinational corporations,
love of neighbor necessarily involves not only interpersonal
and social love, but also political love. The stories and songs of
female slaves are not only words of courage, but words that
challenge the racist structures of society—then and now—
testimonies that call us to awareness of our own complicity and
to conversion. Remembrance of the deaths of the martyrs of El
Salvador calls into question who was responsible for those
deaths and the deaths of countless others, and what economic
and political policies allowed both murders and cover-ups.
Helen Prejean's compassion for a single prisoner on death row
gradually drew her into organized efforts to oppose the death
penalty and to move Catholic leaders, including bishops and

the pope, to condemn the death penalty. Those who hear the voices of women in battered women's shelters or who listen to the stories of prostitutes often find themselves asking questions about welfare laws, the cycle of poverty, and institutionalized sexism that results in domestic violence and sexual exploitation of women.

In a similar dynamic, women who have experienced a serious illness threatening them or someone they love challenge the patterns of the ever-demanding workplace that leaves no room for solitude and leisure, time with family, cultivating relationships, or even basic healthcare. They speak courageously about what really matters in life and, when possible, work for change in the workplace, health-care systems, and beyond. Speaking from her own experience of the connection between women's multiple experiences of suffering and the authority of their words, Audre Lorde, the black lesbian poet, offered the following testimony and challenge to her professional colleagues after her diagnosis of breast cancer:

> In becoming forcibly and essentially aware of my mortality, and of what I wished and wanted for my life, however short it might be, priorities and omissions became strongly etched in a merciless light, and what I most regretted were my silences. Of what had I *ever* been afraid? To question or to speak as I believed could have meant pain, or death. But we all hurt in so many different ways, all the time, and pain will either change or end. Death, on the other hand, is the final silence. And that might be coming quickly, now, without regard for whether I had ever spoken what needed to be said, or had only betrayed myself into small silences, while I planned someday to speak, or waited for someone else's words. And I began to recognize a source of power within myself that comes from the

knowledge that while it is most desirable not to be afraid, learning to put fear into a perspective gave me great strength.[45]

Speaking unwelcome words, naming difficult truths, raising questions, protesting policies, organizing resistance, and working and praying for healing and change are all dimensions of the politics of compassion in our day. As Jon Sobrino has reminded us, standing in solidarity with the crucified of this world involves a commitment to "bring down from the cross those crucified on it."[46] Solidarity also involves the discerning vision and prudence that allow one to read the signs of the times with clarity and to judge accurately one's own role in a given situation. For those who are suffering in a situation of injustice, the challenge to embrace the cross calls for courage and active resistance, rather than passive surrender. But for those who benefit from the unequal distribution of wealth or status or power—including women from dominant groups and cultures—conversion requires divestment and repentance, taking on the struggle of those who suffer within the system, and actively working to change it for the benefit of the common good.

The energy to stay committed to the neighbor in need—to remain at the bedside of the sick, to stay in conversation with a difficult friend or family member, and to keep engaged in what appear to be fruitless efforts for justice in church or society—requires the conviction that more than human effort is at work. Catherine's exhortation to join one's wounds with the wounds of Jesus was grounded in her unflinching conviction that the power of love had overcome the powers of evil and death in the death and resurrection of Jesus. Hers was not a masochistic or passive spirituality. On the contrary, she operated out of what Schillebeeckx has called "grace-optimism"—the conviction that despite all the evidence to the contrary, God's Spirit of mercy is at work in our world and in our lives, empowering us to be ministers of compassion and healing.

Birth of Hope and Courage in the Darkness

But that conviction did not spare her from her own experiences of darkness, doubt, and failure, or her own need to experience compassion. That too was part of her experience of participation in the wounds of the one who died clinging to God while God remained silent. This political mediator sometimes acted naively, was the subject of gossip and criticism, made mistakes, was betrayed and manipulated by others, knew her own sinfulness, and failed in her efforts to bring peace and unity to the Italian city-states. This wise counselor of pontiffs and advocate of church unity died with the church in schism. This woman who wrote so powerfully of the divine physician who offers us healing and used such rich food imagery to describe the Eucharist lived with a severe eating disorder that became irreversible and hastened her death. This saint who experienced a union with God described as "mystical espousal" died questioning what God was doing with her and learned from experience what it means to entrust one's life to God in the darkness.[47]

Perhaps it is precisely here—in her fragility and brokenness—that we can recover a final connection between the authority of Catherine's speech and the authority of solidarity in suffering. Catherine of Siena was a woman "acquainted with grief" from the pain of her own body to the pain of the body of Christ and the body politic. Her questions and assumptions may not always be ours, but the words she spoke, believed, and lived, came from sharing the struggles and pain of the human condition. Her wisdom developed from her experience of chronic illness; from the daily life struggles of families—including her

115

own; from nursing plague victims and feeding the poor; from counseling political prisoners and keeping vigil with them to the end. Her wisdom deepened in searching for a word of encouragement for those who turned to her for advice; in political struggles for peace and reconciliation even when they appeared fruitless; in her bouts of loneliness in the absence of friends; in praying and working for the church to become more fully the body of Christ. She learned from experience that the contemplative wisdom she wanted to seek in the seclusion of her room was to be found in turning to the neighbor in need.

In embracing what God holds dear in creation and the incarnation, Catherine discovered the one whose name is Mercy, the God who loves us "unspeakably much." Her letters, her *Dialogue*, and her relationships reflected that love and joy. But that discovery was not always her experience. She shared the experience of self-doubt and confusion. She wrestled with her own inner demons. In her *Dialogue* she confesses that "my life has been spent wholly in darkness." Yet she remained convinced of God's presence in spite of the darkness, trusting that even there God was affirming her life in spite of her very real limitations and even failures: "But you did what you should have done and what my goodness gave you strength to do—for my goodness is never hidden from anyone who wants to receive it." Catherine described her struggle with fear, confusion, and the possibility that her life was a delusion, but she attributed that radical self-doubt to the work of the devil rather than of God, an insight that contemporary feminist writers on women's journeys of conversion echo heartily.[48]

Without glorifying suffering, we can see Catherine of Siena's authority of compassionate courage reflected in women who have known very different forms of suffering in our own day. Women's voices of authority are as varied as those of Thea Bowman, Maya Angelou, Etty Hillesum, Theresa Kane, Mother Teresa, Helen Prejean, Dolores Huerta, Mamphela Ramphele, of Eileen Egan, of Dorothy Day, of Jane Goodall, the Madres de Plaza de Mayo, Margaret Anna Cusack and other founders of religious orders, our mothers and grandmothers, our teachers and mentors, and countless women of wisdom in each of our lives and memories. Their authority emerged in part from the undeniable fact that they have known suffering—in their own bodies, in their families and countries, in the religious bodies to which they belong. Women's courage to speak from their experience of love and of suffering comes from their own bodies and from the often marginal places in the political, social, and ecclesial bodies of which they are an integral, if often unrecognized, part. Women know from their experience, as did Catherine of Siena in her multivalent symbol of the "blood of Jesus," that in a world of sin, love and suffering are intertwined. They know, too, the power of God at work in their lives and families and communities, sustaining them and opening up unexpected possibilities of reconciliation and hope. Both the life and the death that they have experienced are sources of knowledge and grace for the body of Christ and the body politic.

The experiences from which women speak include bodily experiences of love and well-being as well as of pain and threat; spiritual experiences of light and mystical union as well as darkness and desolation; interpersonal experiences of love, freedom, and union as well as loss, betrayal, and rejection; social experiences of participation, power, and leadership, as well as exclusion, marginalization, and dismissal; ecological experiences of interrelatedness and synergy as well as chaos and entropy; and religious experience of mystical communion as well as the dark night. Women's participation in the body of Christ includes all of those dimensions. Women speak with authority—with depth, freedom, authenticity, and wisdom—when they speak with compassion of the truth that emerges from their experience.

Conclusion

We began by asking what it means for women to identify themselves as full participants in the body of Christ and to speak and act out of that identity. Catherine of Siena stands as one witness to the mysterious ways in which the Spirit conforms faithful women and men to the image of Christ. In the uniqueness of her life journey, Catherine's vocation unfolded as testimony to the fact that in every age Wisdom's prophets are called to preach good news, to order things rightly, and to draw others into communion with God and with one another. The authority to exercise those ministries comes from the source of all authority and all ministries—the Holy Spirit.

There are women today as well who experience a desire and a call to be engaged in building up God's reign on earth in ways they often could not have imagined. At the intersection of their gifts of personality and grace with the unique needs of their time and place, they discover a sense of vocation and energy for mission that impels them to speak and act. Whether their words are recognized or resisted, women in the tradition of Mary Magdalene and Catherine of Siena speak from and about their experience of God. They talk to other women around kitchen tables, they offer advice to children and family members, they encourage others, they listen, they console, they challenge. And like Mary Magdalene and Catherine of Siena, women are called to exercise those same gifts in places where they have not been expected or welcomed in the past—in pulpits, in schools of theology, in board rooms and barrios, in government, in seminaries and universities, in courtrooms, in soup kitchens, in battered women's shelters, in political negotiations, in retreat houses and centers of spirituality, in prisons and hospitals, and in gatherings of the church at every level.

Whatever the setting, those who share Catherine's charism of wisdom are called to speak the truth in love. The authority of the words they speak, even when they do so from official positions of leadership, derives from the truth of their words and the truth of their lives. The charism of wisdom is a gift of the Spirit not limited to the early church or the mystics. Wisdom grants the kind of experience of God that overflows in creative prayer and inspired preaching, in insightful teaching and original theology, in sound counsel and discerning spiritual direction, in prudent judgment and skilled negotiation. No one member of the body of Christ has all the gifts necessary for the vitality of the whole body. Those called to leadership are called to foster dialogue and discernment precisely in the service of the truth to which the whole body is called to be obedient. All of the members of the body are called to participate in the search for truth by speaking the truth in love, living in right relationship, and fostering a climate of truth-telling and listening.

But both the members and the structures of the church are marked by sin as well as by grace. The truth that will make us free will also make us change if we are to be conformed more closely to the one who embodied the truth of God's love for humankind and the cosmos. In the face of our betrayals, both large and small, Wisdom sends forth her prophets to call us to the truth. The ministry of speaking prophetic words is dangerous, both for the prophet and for the community. The prophet remains limited, even sinful, and communities resist change. The exercise of prophetic speech by an individual or a community requires self-knowledge, an ongoing openness to conversion, and compassionate judgment. Here Catherine serves as a companion in hope who held her love of the church and her prayer for its unity in creative tension with her frank assessment of its need for reform.

Catherine's writings remind us, too, that the gifts of prophecy and wisdom are not bestowed only on rare individuals; rather the Spirit bestows multiple gifts on the many members of communities of faith and on all of humankind and creation precisely so that we will realize our need for one another. When the gifts the Spirit has bestowed on any members of the body are denied, minimized, or not exercised, the whole body suffers. When women's imaging of Christ is unrecognized or denied, when women's words of faith and compassion are silenced or limited, the church's witness as sacrament of salvation is compromised. When women such as Catherine freely embrace their apostolic vocations and respond to the needs of their times with words of grace and truth, the Spirit expands our imagination of what the reign of God is like and who is called to announce that reign.

Women today can indeed take hope and courage from Catherine of Siena, who embraced a mission that was not of her making, nor even within her imagination. Amid plague and wars, poverty and papal politics, hunger for survival and hunger for the word of God, she heard a call to do what women did not do. She embraced a vocation to preach on hillsides and to the curia, to pray in the classic language of the church and in words that had the authority of only her experience, to share the mission of her brother preachers when women of the word were supposed to be enclosed in monasteries. She initiated a ministry of peacemaking in a world of politics where she had little expertise; she took stands in complex political situations. When she could not see the way forward, she nevertheless voiced words of protest to family and friends, to world and church: this cannot go on. Even as a young woman, she gathered friends and disciples and shared with them the unspeakable joy of God's love. Without the appropriate education or titles, she authored letters that changed people's lives and became classics of Italian literature. The theological and mystical classic for which she has been recognized as Doctor of Wisdom reflects the riches of the tradition, but also adds new insights to that same tradition. The scriptures and the liturgy of the church formed her into both devoted disciple and keen critic.

And like the one whose life she imaged, Catherine of Siena met resistance, saw her mission fail and her dreams unrealized. She wrestled with her own demons, and died in darkness, clinging to her belief in a compassionate God. Here too she remains companion in hope. Throughout her life she resisted evil and injustice, she spoke and acted with authority, she effected change in world and church. Her courage and her hope were active and evident. Grounded in a contemplative intimacy with God, she persisted in preaching the word in the face of resistance and setbacks. In the end, that same hope sustained her in darkness and pain and the final letting go. Like many other faithful women around the globe, this woman handed on wisdom in her living and in her dying. Her memory remains a source of power and hope, of energy and challenge, for women, for men, and for the church.

Notes

Introduction

1. Pope Paul VI, "Catherine of Siena: The Gift of Wisdom," *The Pope Speaks* 15 (1970): 196–202.

2. Letter 16 to a great prelate, in *The Letters of Catherine of Siena*, Vol. II, translated with introduction and notes by Suzanne Noffke (Tempe, AZ: Arizona Center for Medieval and Renaissance Studies, 2001), 113–18, at 117.

3. On these issues see, for example, Margaret A. Farley, "The Church in the Public Forum: Scandal or Prophetic Witness?" *Proceedings of the Catholic Theological Society of America* 55 (2000): 87–101; Joseph Cardinal Bernardin, "Called to Be Catholic: Church in a Time of Peril," Catholic Common Ground News Conference, August 12, 1996, at http://www.nplc.org/commonground/calledcatholic.htm; Donald B. Cozzens, *Sacred Silence: Denial and the Crisis in the Church* (Collegeville, MN: Liturgical Press, 2002), also *Faith That Dares to Speak* (Collegeville, MN: Liturgical Press, 2004); Paul Lakeland, *The Liberation of the Laity: In Search of an Accountable Church* (New York: Continuum, 2003); Bradford Hinze, *Practices of Dialogue in the Roman Catholic Church: Aims and Obstacles, Lessons and Laments* (New York: Continuum, 2006); M. Shawn Copeland, "Political Theology as Interruptive," *Proceedings of the Catholic Theological Society of America* 59 (2004): 71–82; Peter C. Phan, "'Reception' or 'Subversion' of Vatican II by the Asian Churches: A New Way of Being Church in Asia," *Australian E-Journal of Theology* 6 (February 2006); Margaret O'Brien Steinfels, "What Catholic Women Want," *Boston College Magazine*, Fall 2003; Peter Steinfels, *A People Adrift: The Crisis of the Roman Catholic Church in America* (New York: Simon and Schuster, 2003); James Muller and Charles Kenny, *Keep the Faith and Change the Church: The Battle by Catholics for the Soul of Their Church* (New York: St. Martin's Press, 2004);

Colleen Griffiths, ed., *Guidelines for Prophetic Witness: Catholic Women's Strategies for the Church* (New York: Crossroad, 2008); Pope John Paul II, Apostolic Exhortation, *"Ecclesia in Oceania,"* 22 November 2001, at http://www.vatican.va/holy_father/john_paul_ii/apost_exhortations/documents/hf_jp-ii_exh_20011122_ecclesia-in-oceania_en.htm, accessed on 17 January 2007; "First Sunday of Lent 'Day of Pardon,'" 12 March 2000, at http://www.vatican.va/news_services/liturgy/documents/ns_lit_doc_20000312_presentation-day-pardon_en.html, accessed on 17 January 2007; United States Conference of Catholic Bishops, *Charter for the Protection of Children and Young People*, Revised Edition (Washington, DC, 2002), available at www.nccuscc.org/bishops/charter.htm.

4. *Decree on Ecumenism (Unitatis Redintegratio)*, 21 November 1964, No. 1. Available on the Web at http://www.vatican.va/archive/hist_councils/ii_vatican_council/documents/vat-ii_decree_19641121_unitatis-redintegratio_en.html, accessed on 13 January 2007.

5. See transcripts from "Religions and Cultures: The Courage of Dialogue," a conference held at Georgetown University in Washington, DC, on April 26–27, 2006, at http://prayerforpeace.georgetown.edu/, accessed on 17 January, 2007; "The Millennium World Peace Summit of Religious and Spiritual Leaders: Commitment to Global Peace," at http://www.millenniumpeacesummit.com/resources/mwps/Commitment%20to%20Global%20Peace.pdf, accessed on 17 January 2007; *"Dabru Emet:* A Jewish Statement on Christians and Christianity," at http://www.icjs.org/what/njsp/dabruemet.html, accessed on 15 January 2007; Pope Benedict XVI, "Meeting with Representatives of Some Muslim Communities," Cologne, 20 August 2005, and John Paul II, "Address to Moslem Youth," Morocco, 19 August 1985, at http://www.vatican.va/holy_father/john_paul_ii/speeches/1985/august/documents/hf_jp-ii_spe_19850819_giovani-stadio-casablanca_en.html, accessed on 13 January 2007. See also the Web sites of the Community of Sant'Egidio at http://www.santegidio.org/en/ and Pax Christi International at http://www.paxchristi.net/.

6. See the Christian Scholars Group on Christian-Jewish Relations, "A Sacred Obligation: Rethinking Christian Faith in Relation to Judaism and Jewish People," at http://www.bc.edu/research/cjl/meta-elements/sites/partners/csg/Sacred_Obligation.htm, accessed on 15 January 2007; *"Dabru Emet:* A Jewish Statement about

Christians and Christianity"; Eugene B. Borowitz, "A Nearness in Difference: Jewish-Catholic Dialogue Since Vatican II," *Commonweal* CXXXIII/1 (January 13, 2006): 17–20; Mary C. Boys, ed., *Seeing Judaism Anew: Christianity's Sacred Obligation* (Lanham, MD: Rowman and Littlefield Publishers, Inc., 2005), and Tikva Frymer-Kensky, David Novak, Peter Ochs, David Fox Sandmel, and Michael Signer, eds., *Christianity in Jewish Terms* (Boulder, CO: Westview Press, 2000). Other valuable resources on this topic are available at the Boston College Center for Christian-Jewish Learning Web site at http://www.bc.edu/research/cjl/.

7. See, for example, John T. Pawlikowski and Judith Banki, "Praying for the Jews: Two Views on the New Good Friday Prayers," *Commonweal* 135/5 (March 14, 2008).

8. For the revised text of the pope's speech, see Benedict XVI, "Faith, Reason, and the University: Memories and Reflections," 12 September 2006, at http://www.vatican.va/holy_father/benedict_xvi/speeches/2006/september/documents/hf_ben-xvi_spe_20060912_university-regensburg_en.html, accessed on 13 January 2007. The outrage focused on the pope's citation of the Persian emperor Paleologus's claim: "Show me just what Mohammed brought that was new, and there you will find things only evil and inhuman, such as his command to spread by the sword the faith."

9. Ibid., p. 5, n. 3.

10. "Address of His Holiness Benedict XVI to the Ambassadors of Countries with a Muslim Majority and to the Representatives of Muslim Communities in Italy," 25 September 2006, p. 1, at http://www.vatican.va/holy_father/benedict_xvi/speeches/2006/september/documents/hf_ben-xvi_spe_20060925_ambasciatori-paesi-arabi_en.html, accessed on 15 January 2007. Nevertheless, as Francis Clooney and others have noted, the conciliatory statements from the pope and the Vatican focused on how the pope's speech had been received or misinterpreted, rather than on the problematic choice to use the citation in the first place. See Francis X. Clooney, "Learning to Listen: Benedict XVI and Interreligious Dialogue," *Commonweal*, (January 12, 2007): 11–15, at 12.

11. "Open Letter to Pope Benedict XVI," October 12, 2006, published in *Islamica Magazine*, at http://www.islamicamagazine.com/online-analysis/open-letter-to-his-holiness-pope-benedict-xvi.html, accessed on 13 January 2007.

12. "God's Earth Is Sacred: An Open Letter to Church and Society in the United States," February 14, 2005, p. 4 at http://www.nccusa.org/news/14.02.05theologicalstatement.html, accessed on 13 January 2007.

13. Ibid.

14. "Women 2000: Gender Equality, Development, and Peace for the Twenty-First Century," June 5–9, 2000. Fact sheet from the United Nations Department of Public Information in 2000, reprinted on the Internet at http://www.un.org/womenwatch/.

15. Ibid. For further discussion of this, see the chapters by Maria Pilar Aquino, M. Shawn Copeland, Mary Catherine Hilkert, and Elsa Tamez in *The Option for the Poor in Christian Theology*, ed. Daniel G. Groody (Notre Dame, IN: University of Notre Dame Press, 2007).

16. See, for example, *The Church Women Want: Catholic Women in Dialogue*, ed. Elizabeth A. Johnson (New York: Crossroad, 2002).

17. "Prayers for women's ordination draws bishops fire—Church Notes—World Day of Prayer for Women's Ordination," *Catholic New Times*, 20 April 2003, at http://bcm.bc.edu/issues/summer_2004/features.html, accessed on 28 September 2006.

18. "St. Catherine of Siena," Women Priests: The Case for Ordaining Women in the Catholic Church, Internet Library at http:www.womenpriests.org/called/siena.asp, accessed on 28 September 2006.

19. Dorothy Day, *Catholic Worker*, May 1973, as quoted by Mark and Louise Zwick, "Saint Catherine of Siena: A Woman Who Influenced Her Times," *Houston Catholic Worker*, at http://www.cjd.org/paper/roots/rsiena.html, accessed on 28 September 2006.

20. See the cautions of Suzanne Noffke in "Catherine of Siena and Ecclesial Obedience," *Spirituality Today* 41 (1989): 4–17; also in *Catherine of Siena: Vision Through a Distant Eye* (Collegeville, MN: Liturgical Press, 1996), 54–64.

21. See Pope John Paul II, *Mulieris Dignitatem*, "On the Dignity and Vocation of Women," *Origins* 18/17 (October 6, 1988): 262–83.

22. "Interview of the Holy Father Benedict XVI in Preparation for the Upcoming Journey to Bavaria" (September 9–14, 2006), 5 August 2006, p. 5 (of 7), at http://www.vatican.va/holy_father/benedict_xvi/speeches/2006/august/documents/hf_ben-xvi_spe_20060805_intervista_en.html, accessed on 28 September 2006.

23. Ibid. The inclusion of Mary Magdalene is significant here. See chapter 1 for discussion of Mary Magdalene's role as the first witness to the resurrection and as *apostola apostolorum.*

24. Elizabeth A. Johnson, *Friends of God and Prophets: A Feminist Theological Reading of the Communion of Saints* (New York: Continuum, 1998), 215.

25. The image of the fourteenth century as a "distant mirror" for the contemporary era was suggested by Barbara Tuchman in 1978. See Barbara W. Tuchman, *A Distant Mirror: The Calamitous 14th Century,* 1st trade ed. (New York: Knopf, 1978).

1. The Authority of Vocation

1. Noffke, *Catherine of Siena: Vision Through a Distant Eye,* 2.

2. *Libellus de Supplemento* III, vi, iv, 386, as cited in *The Prayers of Catherine of Siena,* ed. Suzanne Noffke (New York: Paulist Press, 1983), 4–5.

3. For critical analysis of these passages and the issues involved in their interpretation, see Elisabeth Schüssler Fiorenza, *In Memory of Her: A Feminist Theological Reconstruction of Christian Origins* (New York: Crossroad, 1983), 226–33, 285–315; and Margaret Y. MacDonald, "Reading Real Women Through the Undisputed Letters of Paul," and "Rereading Paul: Early Interpreters of Paul on Women and Gender," in *Women and Christian Origins,* eds. Ross Shepherd Kraemer and Mary Rose D'Angelo (New York: Oxford University Press, 1999), 199–220, and 236–53.

4. *Gospel of Mary* 17.18–18.15 as cited in Elaine Pagels, *The Gnostic Gospels* (New York: Random House, 1979), 77–78. For further development, see Karen L. King, "The Gospel of Mary Magdalene," in Elisabeth Schüssler Fiorenza, *Searching the Scriptures: A Feminist Commentary,* Vol. 2 (New York: Crossroad, 1994), 601–34.

5. *Didascalia Apostolorum* 3.6, trans. R. Hugh Connolly (Oxford: Clarendon, 1929), 133. See also *Apostolic Constitutions,* Bk. III, c. 6 in *The Ante-Nicene Fathers,* Vol. 7 (New York: Charles Scribner's Sons, 1926), 427–28. On these texts, see Francine Cardman, "Women, Ministry, and Church Order in Early Christianity," in *Women and Christian Origins,* 300–329.

6. Humbert of Romans, "Treatise on the Formation of Preachers," in *Early Dominicans: Selected Writings,* ed. Simon Tugwell

(New York: Paulist Press, 1982), 223. Thomas Aquinas also cites the disparagement of Eve in his biblical commentary on First Corinthians 14, but rightly attributes the quotation to John Chrysostom, rather than Bernard.

7. Thomas Aquinas, *Summa Theologiae*, II–II, q. 177, aa. 1–2.

8. *Summa Theologiae*, II–II, q. 177, a. 2, obj. 3.

9. *Summa Theologiae*, II–II, q. 177, a. 2, reply. Biblical versification according to Blackfriars' edition of the *Summa Theologiae.*

10. Prayer 19, lines 349–55, in *The Prayers of Catherine of Siena*, ed. and trans. Suzanne Noffke (New York: Paulist Press, 1983), 178–79. All references to the prayers of Catherine of Siena are taken from this volume.

11. *Catherine of Siena: The Dialogue*, trans. Suzanne Noffke (New York: Paulist Press, 1980), #135, p. 277. Cited hereafter as *Dialogue.*

12. Prayer 14, lines 171–82, 187–89, pp. 122–23.

13. Letter to the Abbess of the Monastery of Santa Maria delli Scalzi at Florence (T 86), as cited in Mary Ann Fatula, *Catherine of Siena's Way* (Wilmington, DE: Michael Glazier, 1987), 128.

14. Prayer 10, lines 36–45, p. 79.

15. Eleanor McLaughlin, "Women, Power, and the Pursuit of Holiness in Medieval Christianity," in *Women of Spirit: Female Leadership in the Jewish and Christian Traditions*, eds. Rosemary Radford Ruether and Eleanor McLaughlin (New York: Simon and Schuster, 1979), 115. See also Noffke, *Catherine of Siena: Vision Through a Distant Eye*, 7.

16. Karen Scott, "St. Catherine of Siena, 'Apostola,'" in *Church History* 61 (1992): 37. I am indebted to Scott for the material on Catherine as apostle. All references to citations from Catherine's letters in Scott's articles are Scott's original translations.

17. *Epistolario*, L. 65, p. 275, as cited by Scott, 37. [Scott cites from two collections of Catherine's letters: *Epistolario*, ed. Eugenio Dupré Theseider, Rome, 1940, Vol. 1 (the critical edition of 88 letters); and *Le Lettere di S. Caterina da Siena*, ed. Piero Misciattelli, Florence, 1940, 6 vols. (a reworking of Niccolò Tommasèo's collection)]. References to the letters that include volume and page number refer to Misciattelli's collection and use the Tommasèo numeration.

18. *Lettere*, T121, 2:200, as cited by Scott, 39. For the use of these terms to describe male preachers see Humbert of Romans,

"Treatise on the Formation of Preachers," I.2, III.8, IV.29, and XII.135; pp. 184, 187, 193, and 223.

19. Lettere, T122, 2:206, as cited by Scott, "St Catherine of Siena, '*Apostola*,'" 41.

20. Letter to Daniela da Orvieto T316. November 1378, in *The Letters of Catherine of Siena*, Vol. 3, trans. Suzanne Noffke (Tempe, AZ: Arizona Center for Medieval and Renaissance Studies, 2007), 328–31, at 330–31. Catherine does say that she is going to Rome to fulfill the will of the vicar of Christ, but specifically identifies it with "the will of Christ crucified," which is what she has exhorted Daniela to embrace.

21. Lettere, T165, 3:45–46, as cited in Scott, 42.

22. Lettere, T117, 2:185, cited in Scott, 43.

23. Karen Scott notes that in her letters Catherine was silent about being a woman engaging in prophetic and political activities ("'Io Catarina': Ecclesiastical Politics and Oral Culture in the Letters of Catherine of Siena," in *Dear Sister: Medieval Women and the Epistolary Genre*, eds. Karen Cherewatuk and Ulrike Wiethaus [Philadelphia: University of Pennsylvania Press, 1993], 87–121, at 113). Claudia Rattazzi Papka concurs and argues that Catherine circumvented misogyny by not referring to herself as a woman in her letters. ("The Written Woman Writes: Caterina da Siena Between History and Hagiography, Body and Text," *Annali d'Italianistica* 13 [1995]:131–47.) Thomas Luongo attributes to Catherine a far more self-constructed, political, and manipulative use of gender imagery. See "Catherine of Siena: Rewriting Female Authority," in *Women, the Book and the Godly*, eds. Lesley Smith and Jane H. M. Taylor (Cambridge, England: D. S. Brewer, 1995), 89–103; and idem., *The Politics of Marginality: Catherine of Siena in the War of Eight Saints (1374–78)* (PhD diss., University of Notre Dame, 1997).

24. Note Suzanne Noffke's observation based on her work in translating Catherine's writings: "[T]here are ways in which Catherine was, in tune with her age, glaringly sexist in her attitudes, and though I have translated, for example, her *virilmente* (legitimately) as 'courageously,' for her the word definitely carried overtones of 'manliness' as such." Introduction to *Dialogue*, 21.

25. Raymond of Capua, *The Life of Catherine of Siena*, no. 121, translation by Suzanne Noffke.

26. Ibid, no. 122.

27. *Inter Insigniores*, "Vatican Declaration: Women in the Ministerial Priesthood," *Origins* 6/33 (February 3, 1977): #5, p. 522.

28. John Paul II, *Mulieris Dignitatem*, 279.

29. Pope John Paul's "Letter to Women" in 1995 at the time of the Beijing Conference also speaks of the church's need to respect and promote the diverse personal and communal charisms that the Spirit of God bestows for the building up of the Christian community and the good of humanity, but continues to refer to "a certain diversity of roles" that is not an arbitrary imposition, but "rather an expression of what is specific to being male and female." *Origins* 25/9 (July 27, 1995): #11, p. 142.

30. Leon Joseph Cardinal Suenens, *A New Pentecost?* trans. Francis Martin (New York: The Seabury Press, 1975), xii.

31. Aidan Kavanagh, "Unfinished and Unbegun Revisited: The Rite of Christian Initiation of Adults," *Worship* 53 (1979): 327–40, at 330–31.

32. Ibid., 337.

33. Pope Paul VI, "Catherine of Siena: The Gift of Wisdom." See Introduction, n.1.

2. The Authority of Wisdom

1. B. Forshaw, "Doctor of the Church," *New Catholic Encyclopedia*, Vol. 4 (New York: McGraw Hill, 1967), 939.

2. Pope Paul VI, "Teresa of Avila: The Message of Prayer," *The Pope Speaks* 15 (1970): 218–22, at 218.

3. Letter to Pope Gregory XI (T255), 18–22 June 1376, in *The Letters of Catherine of Siena*, Vol. 2, trans. Suzanne Noffke (Tempe, AZ: Medieval and Renaissance Texts and Studies, 2001), 192–94, at 193.

4. Letter to Pope Gregory XI (T206), March 1376, in *The Letters of Catherine of Siena*, Vol. 2, 61–64, at 63–64.

5. Lettere, T267, 4:146, cited by Scott, "Catherine of Siena, 'Apostola,'" 41.

6. Noffke, *Catherine of Siena: Vision Through a Distant Eye*, 62.

7. Prayer 12, lines 127–31, p. 102.

8. Elizabeth A. Johnson, "Jesus, the Wisdom of God: A Biblical Basis for a Non-Androcentric Christology," in *Ephemerides Theologiae Lovanienses* LXI (1985): 275. See also Elisabeth Schüssler Fiorenza, *In*

Memory of Her: A Feminist Reconstruction of Christian Origins (New York: Crossroad, 1983), 132–33.

9. Augustine, *De Trinitate*, VII, 2. PL 42, 936. Lom. 5, 1.45; 27, 3, 174; Thomas Aquinas, *Summa Theologiae* Ia, q. 34, 1, ad. 2 and q. 39, 8, ad. 3. For one example of Catherine's use of the title see Prayer 10, lines 1–23, p. 78.

10. Sequence for Pentecost, translation by Doris Regan, OP.

11. Kathleen M. O'Connor, *The Wisdom Literature* (Wilmington, DE: Michael Glazier, 1988), 70.

12. Thomas Aquinas, *Summa Theologiae*, II–II, q. 45, a. 5, reply; and q. 45, a. 6, obj. 2.

13. See *Summa Theologiae* I, q. 43, a. 5. ad 2; II–II, q. 45, a. 1, reply and ad. 2; II–II, q. 45, a. 2, reply; II–II, q. 45, a. 3, ad. 1; II–II, q. 45, a. 4, reply.

14. Raymond of Capua, *The Life of Catherine of Siena*, trans. Conleth Kearns (Wilmington, DE: Michael Glazier, 1980), #216, p. 205.

15. *Dialogue*, #61, p. 116.

16. Letter to Pope Urban VI (T306) as cited by Noffke in *Catherine of Siena: Vision Through a Distant Eye*, 21.

17. Letter to Pope Gregory XI (T185), January 1376, in *The Letters of St. Catherine of Siena*, Vol. I, trans. Suzanne Noffke (Tempe, AZ: Arizona Center for Medieval and Renaissance Studies, 2000), 244–51, at 245–46.

18. *Dialogue*, #121–133, pp. 231–76.

19. Letter to Pope Gregory XI (T206), March 1376, in *The Letters of St. Catherine of Siena*, Vol. 2, 61–64, at 61–62.

20. Letter to the Elders of Lucca, January–March 1376, in *The Letters of St. Catherine of Siena*, Vol. I, 239–43, at 242–43.

21. Letter to Charles V, King of France (T235), August 1376, in *The Letters of St. Catherine of Siena*, Vol. 2, 219–23, at 220–22.

22. Letter to her brother Benincasa (T18), late 1373 to early 1374, in *The Letters of St. Catherine of Siena*, Vol. I, 31–33, at 33.

23. Karen Scott, "Candied Oranges, Vinegar, and Dawn: The Imagery of Conversion in the Letters of Caterina of Siena," *Annali d'Italianistica: Women Mystic Writers* 13 (1995): 91–107, at 105. Scott's analysis is based on Letter T346 to Pope Urban VI.

24. *Dialogue*, #120, p. 230.

25. *Dialogue*, #7, p. 38.

26. Noffke, *Catherine of Siena: Vision Through a Distant Eye*, 58.

27. Letter to Bernabò (DT17), p. 69, as quoted in Noffke, "Ecclesial Obedience," 7.

28. Letter to Pope Urban VI (T302), translation by Suzanne Noffke, unpublished Vol. IV of *The Letters of Catherine of Siena*. For reference to the council of the servants of God, see Prayer 12, lines 174–78, p. 103, and Noffke's note in *The Prayers of Catherine of Siena*, 106, n. 11.

29. P. Francis Murphy, "Let's Start Over: A Bishop Appraises the Pastoral on Women," *Commonweal*, September 25, 1992, p. 12.

30. See Congregation for the Clergy, "The Priest: Teacher of the Word, Minister of the Sacraments, and Leader of the Community," *Origins* 29/13 (September 9, 1999): 202, and Eight Vatican Offices, "Instruction: On Certain Questions Regarding the Collaboration of the Nonordained Faithful in the Sacred Ministry of Priests," *Origins* 27/24 (November 27, 1997): *passim*.

31. Sister Theresa Kane, RSM, "Welcome to Pope John Paul II," October 7, 1979, from the Archives of the Leadership Conference of Women Religious, CLCW 54/47, University of Notre Dame Archives, Notre Dame, IN.

32. See the Archives of the Leadership Conference of Women Religious, Correspondence 1979–80, CLCW 36/7, and Consortium Perfectae Caritatis, Administrative Meeting, Nov. 14, 1979, CMAS 3/30, University of Notre Dame Archives, Notre Dame, IN.

33. J. M. R. Tillard, "Sensus Fidelium," *One in Christ* 11 (1975): 2–29, at 24.

34. Avery Dulles, "On the Sense of the Faithful," *America* 155 (November 1986): 240–42 and 263, at 241–42.

35. See Sandra M. Schneiders, "Spiritual Discernment in the *Dialogue* of Saint Catherine of Siena," *Horizons* 9/1 (1982): 47–59, and Diana L. Villegas, "Discernment in Catherine of Siena," *Theological Studies* 58 (1997): 19–38. Suzanne Noffke suggests connections between personal discernment and ecclesial processes of discernment in *Catherine of Siena: Vision Through a Distant Eye*, 54–64, and "Catherine of Siena and Ecclesial Obedience."

36. Letter to Cardinal Pedro de Luna (T284), as cited in Noffke, *Catherine of Siena: Vision Through a Distant Eye*, 58.

37. *Dialogue*, #100, pp. 189–90.

38. *Dialogue*, #145, p. 304.

39. *Dialogue*, #11, pp. 44–45.

40. See for example, Margaret O'Brien Steinfels, "The Church and Its Public Life," *America* 160/22 (June 10, 1989): 550–58; Richard A. McCormick, "The Shape of Moral Evasion in Catholicism," *America* 159/8 (October 1, 1988): 183–88; Richard A. McCormick and Richard P. McBrien, "Theology as a Public Responsibility," *America* 165/8 (September 28, 1991): 184–89, 203–6; John R. Quinn, "Considering the Papacy," *Origins* 26/8 (July 18, 1996): 119–28; Kenneth E. Untener, "What a Prophet Does and Does Not Do," *Origins* 21/2 (May 23, 1991): 36–40; Donald B. Cozzens, "Telling the Truth," *The Tablet*, 5 August 2000, 1044–45; idem., *The Changing Face of the Priesthood* (Collegeville, MN: Liturgical Press, 2000); Garry Wills, *Papal Sin: Structures of Deceit* (New York: Doubleday, 2000); and Rosemary Radford Ruether, "Renewed in Zone of Truth," *National Catholic Reporter*, August 25, 2000, p. 16.

41. Katarina Schuth, *Seminaries, Theologates and the Future of Church Ministry* (Collegeville, MN: Liturgical Press, 1999).

42. Letter T344 as cited in Noffke's Introduction to *Dialogue*, 7.

43. Flannery O'Connor, Letter To "A," 20 July 1955, in *The Habit of Being*, ed. Sally Fitzgerald (New York: Farrar, Straus, and Giroux, 1979), 90.

3. The Authority of Compassion

1. See Rudolph Bell, *Holy Anorexia* (Chicago: University of Chicago Press, 1985) and Caroline Walker Bynum, *Holy Feast and Holy Fast: The Religious Significance of Food to Medieval Women* (Berkeley: University of California Press, 1987). On contemporary challenges and possibilities, see Mary Collins, "Is the Eucharist Still a Source of Meaning for Women?" *Origins* 21 (September 12, 1991): 225–29; idem., "Liturgical Spirituality in a Pluralistic Culture," *Doctrine and Life* 41 (1991): 59–67; Susan A. Ross, *Extravagant Affections: A Feminist Sacramental Theology* (New York: Continuum, 1998); idem., "Like a Fish Without a Bicycle?" *America* 181/17 (November 27, 1999): 10–13; and Catherine Vincie, "Eucharist: Satisfying Desires or Feeding Hungers?" paper presented at "Eucharist without Walls." Conference sponsored by Center of Pastoral Liturgy, University of Notre Dame, June 20, 2000.

2. On this point, see Anne Carr, *Transforming Grace: Christian Tradition and Women's Experience* (San Francisco: Harper and Row, 1988), 174–75, Rosemary Radford Ruether, "Christology and Feminism: Can a Male Savior Save Women?" in *To Change the World: Christology and Cultural Criticism* (New York: Crossroad, 1981), 45–56, Jacquelyn Grant, "Subjectification as a Requirement for Christological Construction," in *Lift Every Voice: Constructing Christian Theologies from the Underside*, eds. Susan Brooks Thistlethwaite and Mary Potter Engel (San Francisco: Harper and Row, 1990), 201–14, and Delores S. Williams, *Sisters in the Wilderness: The Challenge of Womanist God-Talk* (Maryknoll, NY: Orbis, 1993), 161–67.

3. Letter to Monna Colomba (T166), cited in *Catherine of Siena: Passion for the Truth, Compassion for Humanity*, ed. Mary O'Driscoll (New York: New City Press, 1993), 33.

4. Letter to Caterina di Scetto (T50), cited in O'Driscoll, 27.

5. Letter to Thomas della Fonte (T41; DT IV), cited in O'Driscoll, 25. For examples of references to the "nails of love," see *Dialogue*, #77, p. 143; and Prayer 5, lines 30–32, p. 48.

6. Letter to her brother Benincasa (T18, DT XIV), cited in O'Driscoll, 21.

7. Letter to Sister Eugenia (T26), cited in O'Driscoll, 23.

8. Letter to Raymond of Capua (T344), cited in O'Driscoll, 48.

9. Letter to William Flete and Antonio da Nizza (T326), translation by Suzanne Noffke, unpublished volume IV of *The Letters of Catherine of Siena*.

10. Letter to authorities in Bologna (T268), cited in O'Driscoll, 40.

11. Letter to Pope Gregory XI (T233; DT LXXXVI), cited in O'Driscoll, 38.

12. Letter to Pope Urban VI (T291), cited in O'Driscoll, 47.

13. Letter to Raymond of Capua (T273, DT XXXI), cited in O'Driscoll, 42–43. Luongo's analysis of this letter proposes a complex erotic interpretation of the letter, of Catherine's authority, and of the imagery of the wounds of Jesus. See n. 27.

14. Prayer 1, lines 60–67, p. 17.

15. Prayer 11, lines 225–26, p. 92.

16. Prayer 17, lines 38–40, p. 148.

17. Prayer 17, lines 41–49, p. 148.

18. *Dialogue*, #30, p. 72; see also *Dialogue*, #153, p. 325. For references to God as "drunk with love" or "crazy with love" in Catherine's prayers, see Prayers 10, 13, 17.

19. Prayer 19, lines 252–53, p. 176.

20. *Dialogue*, #126, pp. 245–46.

21. *Dialogue*, #66, p. 124.

22. See Bynum, 177, and M.-D. Chenu, "Sang du Christ," DTC, vol. 14 (1939), cols. 1094–97.

23. *Dialogue*, #14, p. 52. For the Spirit as nursing mother, see *Dialogue*, #141, p. 292.

24. *Dialogue*, #96, p. 180.

25. Bynum, *Holy Feast and Holy Fast*, 179. In his analysis of Catherine's eating disorders, Rudolph Bell places great emphasis on Catherine's guilt related to the death of her twin sister who was sent to a wet-nurse while Catherine was nursed by her own mother. See chap. 3, n. 1.

26. *Dialogue*, #142, pp. 295–96. See also Raymond of Capua, *The Life of Catherine of Siena*, #187, pp. 180–81.

27. *Dialogue*, #76, pp. 140–41.

28. Prayer 14, lines 20–25, p. 118.

29. *Dialogue*, #86, p. 159.

30. Mary Daly, *Beyond God the Father* (Boston: Beacon, 1973), 75–77.

31. See Rita Nakashima Brock, *Journeys by Heart: A Christology of Erotic Power* (New York: Crossroad, 1988); Joanne Carlson Brown and Rebecca Parker, "For God so Loved the World?" in *Christianity, Patriarchy, and Abuse*, eds. Joanne Carlson Brown and Carole R. Bohn (New York: Pilgrim, 1989); Dorothee Soelle, *Suffering*, trans. Everett Kalin (Philadelphia: Fortress, 1976), 26–28; Christian Gudorf, *Victimization: Examining Christian Complicity* (Philadelphia: Trinity Press International, 1992); and Cynthia S. W. Crysdale, *Embracing Travail: Retrieving the Cross Today* (New York: Continuum, 1999).

32. Delores M. Williams, *Sisters in the Wilderness: The Challenge of Womanist God-Talk* (Maryknoll, NY: Orbis, 1993), 167.

33. Elisabeth Schüssler Fiorenza, *Jesus: Miriam's Child, Sophia's Prophet* (New York: Continuum, 1994), 102.

34. M. Shawn Copeland, "'Wading Through Many Troubling Sorrows': Toward a Theology of Suffering in Womanist Perspective," in *A Troubling in My Soul: Womanist Perspectives on Evil and Suffering*, ed.

Emilie M. Townes (Maryknoll, NY: Orbis, 1993), 121. Copeland also cites Joanne M. Braxton, *Black Women Writing Autobiography: A Tradition within a Tradition* (Philadelphia: Temple University Press, 1988).

35. Copeland, "'Wading Through Many Sorrows': Toward a Theology of Suffering in Womanist Perspective," 109–29, at 120.

36. Lydia Lascano, "Women and the Christ Event," in *Proceedings: Asian Women's Consultation* (Manila: EATWOT, 1985): 127, as cited in Chung Hyun Kyung, *Struggle to Be Sun Again: Introducing Asian Women's Theology* (Maryknoll, NY: Orbis, 1990), 63.

37. Final Document: Intercontinental Women's Conference, Oaxtepec, Mexico, December 1–6, 1986, in *With Passion and Compassion: Third World Women Doing Theology*, eds. Virginia Fabella and Mercy Amba Oduyoye (Maryknoll, NY: Orbis, 1988), 184–90, at 188.

38. As quoted by Judith M. Noone, in *The Same Fate as the Poor* (Maryknoll, NY: Orbis, 1984, 1995), 71.

39. Ita Ford, "Reflections on the Mission Phase," May 1977, as quoted in Noone, 82.

40. *Salvador Witness*, 212, as quoted by Sheila Cassidy in *Good Friday People* (Maryknoll, NY: Orbis, 1991), 61.

41. As quoted in Placido Erdozain, *Archbishop Romero, Martyr of Salvador* (Maryknoll, NY: Orbis, 1981), 75.

42. "An Interview with Betty Williams," by Dawn Engle and Ivan Suvanjieff, Houston, Texas, July 4, 1995, reprinted on the Internet at www.peacejam.org., p. 2 of 8.

43. The phrase is taken from Jon Sobrino, "Political Holiness: A Profile," in *Martyrdom Today, Concilium*, Vol. 165, eds. Johannes-Baptist Metz and Edward Schillebeeckx (New York: Seabury, 1983), 18–23.

44. *Dialogue*, #64, p. 121, translation corrected by Noffke.

45. Audre Lorde, "The Transformation of Silence into Language and Action," in *Sister Outsider* (Freedom, CA: The Crossing Press, 1984), 40–44, at 41. For a powerful reflection on the connection between the experience of a woman's healing from breast cancer and the process of healing needed in the church, see Mary Jo Weaver, "Cancer in the Body of Christ," in *Women's Spirituality: Resources for Christian Development*, 2nd edition, ed. Joanne Wolski Conn (New York: Paulist Press, 1996), 68–82.

46. Jon Sobrino, "Evil and Hope: A Reflection from the Victims," *CTSA Proceedings* 50 (1995): 71–84, at 76.

47. See Letter to Raymond of Capua (T373, 4:173–78).

48. *Dialogue,* #66, pp. 124–25. For an overview of the issues involved in women's journeys of conversion, see the related essays in Conn, *Women's Spirituality,* and Fabella and Oduyoye (eds.), *With Passion and Compassion,* as well as Rosemary Radford Ruether, *Sexism and God-Talk* (Boston: Beacon, 1993), 183–92, and Elizabeth Dreyer, *Manifestations of Grace* (Wilmington, DE: Michael Glazier, 1990), 185–89.

green press
INITIATIVE

Paulist Press is committed to preserving ancient forests and natural resources. We elected to print this title on 30% post consumer recycled paper, processed chlorine free. As a result, for this printing, we have saved:

4 Trees (40' tall and 6-8" diameter)
1,398 Gallons of Wastewater
3 million BTU's of Total Energy
180 Pounds of Solid Waste
337 Pounds of Greenhouse Gases

Paulist Press made this paper choice because our printer, Thomson-Shore, Inc., is a member of Green Press Initiative, a nonprofit program dedicated to supporting authors, publishers, and suppliers in their efforts to reduce their use of fiber obtained from endangered forests.

For more information, visit www.greenpressinitiative.org

Environmental impact estimates were made using the Environmental Defense Paper Calculator. For more information visit: www.papercalculator.org.